T4-AJT-391

Creative Bible Activities for Children Series

Life and Lessons of Jesus — Vol. 3

Following Jesus

Copyright © 1991 by Tracy Leffingwell Harrast.
Published by Cook Communications Ministries.

Printed in the United States of America.

All puzzles and Bible activities are based on the NIV.

Scripture taken from the Holy Bible, New International Version, Copyright ©1973, 1978, 1984 International Bible Society. Used by permission of Zondervan Publishing House.

Cover Illustration by Gary Locke

Cover Design by Todd Mock and Mike Riester

Interior Illustrations by Anne Kennedy

Interior Design by Tabb Associates, Mike Riester and Cheryl Morton

ISBN #0781438497   101843

Life and Lessons of Jesus Vol. 3—Following Jesus

CONTENTS

Names of Jesus

Following Jesus

Learning to Love Like Jesus

Names of Jesus

Seek and You Will Find

Find these names of Jesus in the puzzle and circle them.

ALPHA AND OMEGA
BREAD OF LIFE
CHRIST
DELIVERER
IMMANUEL
FRIEND

GATE
I AM
JESUS
KING OF KINGS
LIGHT
MESSIAH

PASSOVER LAMB
REDEEMER
SAVIOR
TEACHER
VINE
WORD

```
L  I  G  H  T  R  G  I  A  M  S  U  S  E  J
C  B  W  O  R  D  V  I  N  E  R  O  I  V  A
R  O  I  V  A  S  N  E  C  S  V  K  L  T  R
P  F  E  S  N  R  B  A  H  S  A  F  L  D  C
A  L  Y  A  R  E  J  K  R  I  M  R  A  E  H
S  D  Y  L  N  O  L  I  I  A  Y  I  U  L  E
S  R  E  H  T  A  E  H  S  H  J  E  R  I  R
O  N  L  Y  B  E  G  O  T  T  E  N  E  V  Y
V  I  M  M  A  N  U  E  L  H  H  D  N  E  L
E  M  Y  C  N  A  N  L  K  S  D  A  B  R  M
R  E  D  E  E  M  E  R  G  I  O  I  T  E  I
L  L  E  R  R  E  T  K  R  A  M  W  E  R  J
A  L  P  H  A  A  N  D  O  M  E  G  A  T  E
M  Y  C  N  A  N  R  O  B  I  N  M  C  L  H
B  R  E  A  D  O  F  L  I  F  E  S  H  G  S
Y  B  U  R  D  L  G  C  N  O  V  D  E  T  O
S  S  G  N  I  K  F  O  G  N  I  K  R  F  J
```

Add a Line

Here's your big chance to be a detective! See if you can figure out what the shapes below say. *Add one line to each of the shapes to form a letter. The letters make names of Jesus. If you need help, look at the contents on pages 3-4 to see some of Jesus' names. Have fun!*

1. ᑕᖴᐤ ᒐᑕᑭ

2. ᒐ᚛ᔕᔕᒐᑎᕼ

3. ᕼᑭᖴᒐᐤ ᒐᕼᕼ ᒐ ᒐᑕᕼ

4. ᕼᖇᒐᕼᐤ

5. ᑕᒐᐤ

6. ᒐ ᑐᖇᐤ

7. ᒐ ᖴᒐᕼ ᕼᑕᒐ ᑕᑐᐤ

8. ᖽᒐᐤᑕᕼᑕ ᖽᑐᐤᑕᔕ

9. ᒐᒐᑕᑭᐤ

10. ᑭᕼᐤᕼᑕᒐᖴᑭ

8   *Life and Lessons of Jesus Vol. 3—Names of Jesus*

Alpha and Omega

Jesus said, "I am the Alpha and the Omega, the First and the Last, the Beginning and the End." Alpha and omega are the first and last letters of the Greek alphabet. In English, Jesus would be saying He is the A and the Z.

Jesus' life didn't begin when He was born in Bethlehem, and it didn't end when He was crucified. Jesus was with the Father when time began, and He will be with the Father when time ends.

Alpha and Omega Book Rack

Jesus knows what's in every book that was ever written. He has seen everything that has happened in the past, and He can see everything that will happen in the future. Make this book rack to remind you of all that Jesus knows.

What You Need

- 2 boxes that are the same size
- scissors
- 2 or more patterns of self-adhesive paper
- pencil
- ruler
- paper

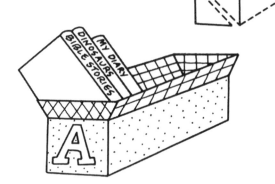

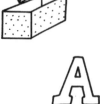

Alpha   Omega

What You Do

1. *On one narrow end of box 1, draw a line from the top left corner to the bottom right corner. On the other narrow end of the box, draw a line from the top right corner to the bottom left corner.*

2. *Cut along the lines and along the crease as shown so that you have a triangle-shaped box.*

3. *Cover both boxes with patterned self-adhesive paper, using a different pattern for each box. Put box 1 inside box 2 as shown.*

4. *Draw an alpha and an omega on self-adhesive paper different from box 2, and cut them out.*

5. *Remove the backing from the alpha and attach it to one end of box 2. Remove the backing from the omega and attach it to the other end of box 2. Now you can fill your rack with books!*

Draw a star in this box when you've read John 1:1-3; and Revelation 11:6, 15; 22:13.

The Bread of Life

After Moses and the Israelites left Egypt, they wandered around in the wilderness for forty years. During that time, God sent a breadlike food called manna from heaven each day to keep them alive. Jesus said that He is the living bread that came down from heaven that will keep us alive for eternity!

Decode three ways that Jesus is like manna.

1. Fill in the missing vowels. The vowels are A, E, I, O, and U.

P_ _pl_   w_nt   t_   kn_w   G_d   _nd   b_   sur_   th_y   w_ll   g_t   t_   l_v_   w_th   H_m   f_r_v_r.   Wh_n   th_y   p_t   th_ _r   tr_st   _n   J_s_s,   H_   s_t_sf_ _s   th_t   h_ng_r   l_k_   th_   m_nn_   s_t_sf_ _d   th_   h_ng_r   _f   th_   _sr_ _l_t_s.

2. It's as easy to read as 1, 2, 3! To find out what these numbers are trying to say, replace each number with the letter that holds its place in the alphabet.
1=A, 2=B, 3=C, 4=D, 5=E, 6=F, 7=G, 8=H, 9=I, 10=J, 11=K, 12=L, 13=M, 14=N, 15=0, 16=P, 17=Q, 18=R, 19=S, 20=T, 21=U, 22=V, 23=W, 24=X, 25=Y, 26=Z

20/8/5   9/19/18/1/5/12/9/20/5/19   23/15/21/12/4   8/1/22/5   4/9/5/4   9/6

7/15/4   8/1/4   14/15/20   19/5/14/20   13/1/14/14/1.   23/5   23/15/21/12/4

1/12/12   4/9/5   6/15/18   5/20/5/18/14/9/20/25   9/6   7/15/4   8/1/4   14/15/20

19/5/14/20   10/5/19/21/19.

3. Looks like someone's typewriter had the hiccups! To decode this message, correct the spacing between the words.

TheIsr aeli teshad toco llect the irma nna ev eryd ay.Wen eedto prayev eryd ayandke ep tr usti nginJe sus.

[ ]   *Draw a star in this box when you've read John 6:31-58.*

Make Bread Words

Jesus said, "I am the bread of life." You can write about the Bread of Life by following this recipe!

What You Need

- grown-up help
- frozen bread dough
- shortening
- egg white
- 1 teaspoon water
- coarse kosher salt

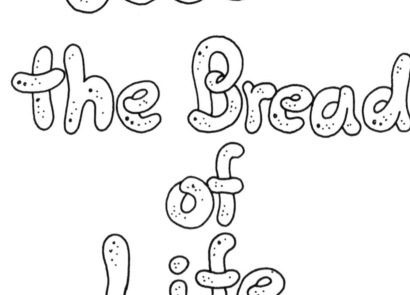

What You Do

1. *Thaw the dough.*

2. *Have a grown-up preheat the oven to the temperature recommended on the bread dough package.*

3. *Shape the dough into letters and put them on a greased cookie sheet.*

4. *Mix the egg white with water and brush onto the letters.*

5. *Sprinkle with coarse kosher salt.*

6. *Bake until golden brown. Watch carefully, because this will bake much faster than the package says it would take for a loaf to bake. (Be sure to have a grown-up help you put your bread into the oven and take it out.)*

☐ *Draw a star in this box when you've read John 6:48.*

The Bridegroom

Jesus called Himself the Bridegroom. A bridegroom is a man who is getting married. In Bible times, people became betrothed before they got married. When they got betrothed, they would make marriage promises and then later they would hold a wedding dinner and celebration.

Jesus is a Bridegroom to everyone who believes in Him. He has promised to come back and take His believers to their new home in heaven, just as a bridegroom takes his bride to live with him. For those who love Jesus, it will be a time of great celebration.

One day Jesus told this story about a wedding feast to show how God calls people to be in His kingdom.

Be Ready for the Bridegroom

Fill in each blank with the correct word from the following list. You can check your answers in Luke 12:35-38.

door
wedding
table
master
lamps
servants
service
knocks
watching
good

Be dressed ready for 1._____ and keep your 2._____ burning, like men waiting for their master to return from a 3._____ banquet, so that when he comes and 4._____ they can immediately open the 5._____ for him. It will be good for those 6._____ whose master finds them 7._____ when he comes. I tell you the truth, he will dress himself to serve, will have them recline at the 8._____ and will come and wait on them. It will be 9._____ for those servants whose 10._____ finds them ready, even if he comes [very late at night].

☐ *Draw a star in this box when you've read Luke 12:35-38.*

The Wedding Feast

A [king] thr+[shoe]-sh A wedding [table] 4 his [son]. The [people] [owl] were invited would [worm] come when the [king]'s helpers went to c+[ball]-B them. They [ha ha ha]+ed [bat]-B the helpers & even killed them! The [king] S+[tent]-T his [arm]+Y 2 [fire] th+[bear]-B city. Then the [king] S+[tent]-T his helpers 2 ask every 1 else 2 the wedding.

1. Which picture in the story was God? Draw it here.

2. Which picture in the story was Jesus? Draw it here.

Draw a star in this box when you've read Matthew 9:15; 22:1-10; Mark 2:19, 20; Luke 5:34, 35.

Ten Young Women with Lamps

In Bible times, people didn't have electric lights like we have today. They filled a lamp with oil and put a wick in it. If there was no oil, the lamp wouldn't burn.

Jesus liked to teach people things by telling them a story. Here is a story He told that has a word missing from each line. To complete the story, put a **∧** mark on each line to show where the word at the beginning of the line belongs. (In line one, the word *ten* belongs before *young*.)

ten	The kingdom of heaven is like young women who took their lamps
wise	and went to meet the bridegroom. Five of them were and five were
oil	foolish. The foolish ones brought lamps without extra, but the wise
asleep	brought oil with their lamps. They all fell waiting for the bridegroom.
Go	At midnight someone yelled, "The bridegroom is coming. out to meet
young	him." All the women got up and cut the wicks on their lamps. The
oil	foolish ones asked the wise ones for some, but the wise women
for	couldn't give them any because there would not be enough everyone.
oil	The foolish young women left to buy some. While they were gone,
came	the bridegroom. The ones who were ready went inside for the wedding,
door	and the was shut behind them. When the foolish young women
the	returned, bridegroom didn't let them inside. He said, "I don't know
day	you." Jesus said for us to watch because we don't know the or hour
	when He'll come.

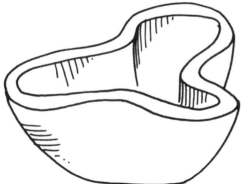

Just as the wise women were ready and waiting for the bridegroom, we can be ready by trusting Jesus as Lord and Savior.

You can make a lamp from clay like the one that Jesus might have been thinking about when He told this story. Keep your lamp in a spot where it will remind you to keep Jesus' light in your life.

Draw a star in this box when you've read Matthew 25:1-13.

The Christ

The Greek word "christ" means "anointed." When someone is anointed, oil is put on that person. Sometimes when people are anointed, it is to show that God has chosen that person for a special purpose, such as becoming a prophet, priest, or king. God chose Jesus to do something no one else could do—take the punishment for our sins and make us ready to live with God forever.

As Christians we get our name from Christ. We are people who believe Jesus is the Christ, the Anointed One. He is our Prophet, Priest, and King.

What is usually used to anoint? Write your answer on the drop.

Make a Bumper Sticker for Your Bike

What You Need

- white Con-Tact paper
- scissors
- permanent markers
- permission from a parent to put the sticker on your bike

What You Do

1. *Be sure you are a Christian. Have you believed and done what is written at the bottom of this page?*
2. *If you are a Christian, make a bumper sticker by cutting a strip of white Con-Tact paper to fit on your bike.*
3. *Use permanent markers to write "I'm a Christian" and draw a cross on the Con-Tact paper.*
4. *Stick it onto your bike's fender.*
5. *When people ask you about your bumper sticker, tell them it means that you believe you are going to heaven because Jesus died for you and that you have promised to obey Him as your Lord. Tell them how they can become Christians, too.*

How to Become a Christian

1. Believe that Jesus is the Christ and want Him to save you and lead you.
2. Pray a prayer like this in your own words:

Dear God,

I believe that Jesus is the Christ. Thank You for sending Him to save me from my sins. I am sorry for the things that I have done wrong. Please forgive me because of Jesus. I have faith in Him as my Savior, and I want to follow Him all of my life as my Lord.

In Jesus' name I pray. Amen.

☐ *Draw a star in this box when you've read Acts 4:27; 10:38; and Hebrews 1:9.*

Commander

It's hard to win a battle if you don't even know you're fighting! Did you know you're in a war? The devil is your enemy. He uses different ways to tempt you to sin, and he tries to prevent you from doing the good that God wants you to do.

Jesus is leading His troops in the battle. In the Bible He is called the Commander of the army of the Lord, a Leader and Commander of the peoples, and the Deliverer.

You're one of His troops if you've asked Him to be your Lord. Listen to Jesus when He tells you how to fight temptations. Obey His commands. In order to win a battle, soldiers in the army need to listen to and obey the instructions of their leader. For Christians to win the war against Satan, we must listen to and obey the directions of our Commander.

Make Military I.D. Tags

People in some armies wear metal tags called "dog tags" to identify themselves.

What You Need

- *3" x 5" index card*
- *ruler*
- *pencil*
- *scissors*
- *small alphabet macaroni*
- *glue*
- *aluminum foil*
- *hole punch*
- *26-inch piece of string*
- *tape*

What You Do

1. *Use a ruler to draw a rectangle about 1 inch by 2 inches on the 3" x 5" card. Fold the card in half and cut out two rectangles at the same time. Round the corners of each rectangle so both have a dog tag shape.*
2. *Arrange macaroni letters to say "I'm in the Lord's army" and glue them onto one dog tag. Arrange letters to spell your name and glue them onto the other dog tag. Let them dry.*
3. *Cover the dog tags with foil. Tape the foil to the back, and carefully rub your finger over the letters on the front so they show.*
4. *Punch a hole in each dog tag and hang them both from the string. Tie the ends of the string into a knot and put the dog tag necklace over your head to show that you're in the army of the Lord!*

Draw a star in this box when you've read Joshua 5:13-15; Isaiah 55:4; Romans 11:26; and Ephesians 6:10-12.

The Chief Cornerstone

If you were going to build a building, the first thing you must have is a foundation. The foundation of the building is the flat part on which the rest of the building is built. The chief cornerstone is the first rock that is put in the foundation and is a very important rock because the building won't stand if the other rocks don't fit with it.

The Lord's church is like a building made of people, and when God built His church, He knew He needed an incredibly perfect cornerstone. Jesus came to earth to be that cornerstone. Even though most of the Jewish leaders and lots of other people didn't believe in Him, He knew and God knew that the church couldn't stand without Him!

Fill in the Foundation

Jesus is the Chief Cornerstone of the house of God, and the rest of the foundation is the apostles and prophets. The things we believe should be based on what they have taught. How many disciples' and prophets' names can you fill in on this foundation? There are many more disciples and prophets than this in the real foundation of God's church, but here are some of them.

J_m_s   J_h_   Th_m_s   Ma__hew   P_u_

E_ij_h   J_n_h   D_ni_l   J_h_   P_t_r

J_su_   N__h   J_seph   M_s_s   Da_i_

You are one of the rocks of Jesus' church. Do you fit with the Cornerstone? Ask yourself these questions to find out.

1. Do the things I believe match what Jesus, the disciples, and the prophets really taught?

2. Am I letting Jesus make me more like Him each day?

☐ *Draw a star in this box when you've read Matthew 21:42; Mark 12:10; Luke 20:17; Acts 4:11; I Corinthians 3:11; Ephesians 2:19-22; and I Peter 2:6.*

Friend

CODE

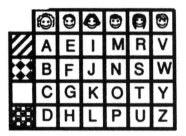

Jesus, the Son of God and Savior of the world, wants to be your friend! To decode what Jesus said about being a friend to you, find each friend's face at the top of the chart and the pattern on his or her shirt at the side of the chart. The column and the row meet at the letter you should write below the friend in the puzzle. For example, 😊 is A.

1. Jesus said, "

_____ _____ _____ _____ _____

 ." (John 15:15)

_____ _____

2. If you feel too guilty to pray, remember: 

_____ _____ _____

  . (Luke 15:1-2)

_____ _____ _____

3. Jesus showed how greatly He loves you, His friend, when

_____ _____

   ." (John 15:13)

_____ _____ _____ _____

4. You are never alone because Jesus said,"

_____ _____ _____

 ." (Matt. 28:20)

_____ _____

☐ *Draw a star in this box when you've read Matthew 28:20; Luke 15:1, 2; and John 15:13, 15.*

The Gate

At night during the cold season, shepherds brought their sheep through a door or gate into a village sheepfold. Everyone, man or sheep, who wanted to enter the safety of the sheepfold had to go through that one door.

Jesus said, "I am the gate; whoever enters through me will be saved." Just as there was only one way to get into the sheepfold, there is only one way for us to get to heaven—Jesus.

Color the sheep with the letters B, D, W, and Z on them. The white sheep will tell you Jesus' message.

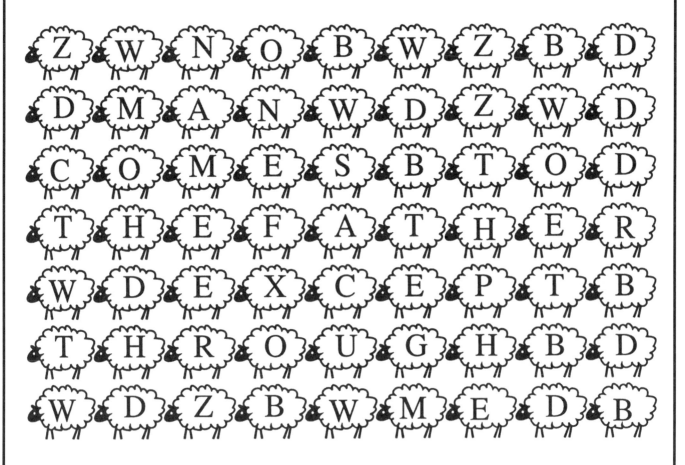

Z W N O B W Z B D
D M A N W D Z W D
C O M E S B T O D
T H E F A T H E R
W D E X C E P T B
T H R O U G H B D
W D Z B W M E D B

Draw a star in this box when you've read John 10:9 and 14:6.

The Gate and Ladders

Jesus said, "I tell you the truth, the man who does not enter the sheep pen by the gate, but climbs in by some other way, is a thief and a robber."

Even though Jesus told us clearly that He is the only way to heaven, people still try all kinds of other ways to get there. Cut out the beliefs at the bottom of the page. Most of them include things that are good to do, but only one of them will save you. Tape the false ideas on the ladders and the true one on the door.

Have you gone through Jesus to enter the kingdom of God? If you have asked Jesus to be your Savior, write your name on one of the sheep in the fold. If you aren't one of His sheep yet, you can become one by putting your trust in Jesus as the only way to get to heaven.

Beliefs to cut out and tape to the ladders and door.

| Being a nice person will save me. | Being a member of my church will save me. | Trusting the leaders of my church will save me. | Attending church will save me. | Being part of a good family will save me. | Trusting Jesus as my way to heaven will save me. |

Draw a star in this box when you've read John 10:1.

Gift of God

Everyone loves to get gifts, and God gave us the best gift of all! To find out more about God's gift, decode the answers to the questions below by finding the letter that has the same pattern as the wrapping paper on each gift.

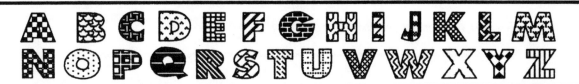

1. When Jesus talked to the woman at the well, He spoke of Himself as what? (John 4:10)

2. Why was God willing to give His one and only son? (John 3:16)

3. A wage is something you earn, but a gift is something given to you. The wage of sin is death, but what is the gift of God? (Romans 6:23)

4. What is our response to God for the gift He's given us? (II Corinthians 9:15)

Draw a star in this box when you've read John 3:16; 4:10; Romans 6:23; and 11.

God

A name is a very important thing; it identifies a person. For the Jewish people, the name of God was a very, very special name. God told Moses His very special name. Many years later, Jesus called Himself the same name that God had told Moses. By doing that, Jesus said that He was God. What was the name that God had called Himself? *Color all of the spaces with dots to find this name.*

1. Circle the number that fills in the blank.
Jesus said He and His Father are _____. (John 10:30)

1   2   3   4   5   6   7   8   9   0

2. Circle the sign that fills in the blank.
Some Jewish people tried to kill Jesus for saying that God was His Father, making Himself ____ with God. (John 5:18)

+   -   =   < >

☐ *Draw a star in this box when you've read Exodus 3:13, 14; John 5:18; 8:58, 59; and 10:30.*

Immanuel

Before Jesus was born, an angel appeared to Joseph in a dream and said that Jesus would be named Immanuel. *To find the meaning of the name in the puzzle below, find the letter each heart is beside. Write it in the box at the bottom of the column. When you have written the letters for all of the hearts, you'll have the meaning of the name Immanuel.*

A B C D E F G H I J K L M N O P Q R S T U V W X Y Z

Immanuel means ___ ___ ___   ___ ___ ___ ___   ___ ___

☐ *Draw a star in this box when you've read Matthew 1:23.*

Jesus

Fill in the blanks and then write your answers in the squares of the puzzle at the bottom of the page. If your answers are right, you will find Jesus' name in the puzzle. When you find it, circle it.

1. "Jesus" is the Greek form of the Hebrew name _ _ _ _ _ _. God chose a man by this name to lead the children of Israel into the promised land of Canaan. The sixth book of the Old Testament is named after him.

2. An _ _ _ _ _ told Joseph in a dream that he should name God's son Jesus.

3. Jesus' name means "The LORD is _ _ _ _ _ _ _ _ _." (The last word of Luke 2:30)

4. This apostle wrote in Philippians 2:9 that Jesus' name is a name above every name. (Look at the first page of Philippians to see who wrote it.) _ _ _ _

5. Jesus is the only name by which people must be _ _ _ _ _. (Acts 4:12).

Draw a star in this box when you've read Matthew 1:20, 21; Luke 2:30; Acts 4:12; and Philippians 2:9.

Make "Stained Glass" for Your Window

What You Need

- colored plastic food wrap (if unavailable, color plain plastic food wrap with permanent markers)
- paper plate
- glue
- string
- scissors
- thread
- tape

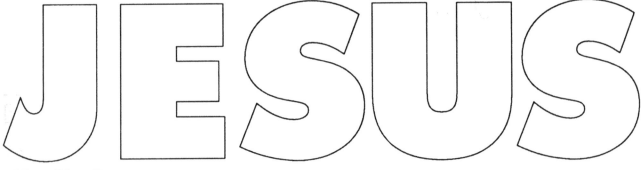

What You Do

1. Tape colored plastic food wrap over the design on this page.
2. Measure and cut a piece of string to cover the lines on the letter "J."
3. Place the string on the plate and cover it with glue.
4. Carefully lay the string on top of the plastic wrap along the lines of the letter.
5. Cut and glue more strings for the rest of the letters in Jesus' name.
6. Let the letters dry completely.
7. Untape the plastic wrap from the page and trim the extra plastic wrap from around each letter.
8. Cut a tiny hole at the top of each letter.
9. Tie a thread through each hole. Hang the letters in your window by taping the threads to the window frame.
- Variation—If you have more than one color of plastic wrap, you could make the letters different colors.

Draw a star in this box when you've read Matthew 1:20, 21; Luke 2:30; Acts 4:12; and Philippians 2:9.

The Kings of Kings

What do you think of when you hear the word "power"? A president? A very rich man? A superhero? God gave Jesus incredible power and authority. Jesus has more power and authority than any king, president, or superhero.

Even though Jesus could force people to obey Him, He lets them choose whether they will or not. Christians are people who choose to let Jesus rule their lives. When people choose to follow Jesus, they become part of His kingdom.

Jesus told many stories of what His kingdom is like. *Write the number of the parable in the box next to the picture it matches.*

1. A man who sowed (planted) good seed. (Matthew 13:24-30, 38-43)

2. A grain of a mustard seed. (Mark 4:30-32)

3. Leaven, yeast, or another substance that makes dough get light and fluffy. (Luke 13:20, 21)

4. A treasure. (Matthew 13:44)

5. A pearl. (Matthew 13:45, 46)

6. A net. (Matthew 13:47-50)

Draw a star in this box when you've read Bible stories about Jesus' kingdom.

A Fun Thing to Do

You can write a book! Find and read one of Jesus' stories about His kingdom. Staple papers together to make a little book. Write the story in the book and illustrate it.

7. A king who forgave a man who owed him money until that man wouldn't forgive another. (Matthew 18:23-35)

8. A man who hired people to work in his grape vineyard at different times in the day and paid them all the same wage. (Matthew 20:1-16)

9. A king who gave a wedding feast for his son. (Matthew 22:2-14)

10. Ten young women with lamps. (Matthew 25:1-13)

11. A man leaving on a trip who gave his workers coins called talents. (Matthew 25:14-30)

The Lamb of God

Before Jesus had died for our sins, God's people sacrificed perfect lambs to God. The lambs were killed for the people's sins. Men called High Priests took the lamb's blood into a room of the temple called the Holy of Holies. One name for Jesus is the Lamb of God. He was the absolutely perfect sacrifice and died for all the sins of the whole world. He acted as the last High Priest for us and went into God's presence to offer Himself as a sacrifice. Because Jesus did this, we no longer need to make sacrifices to God to get rid of our sin—we just ask for forgiveness!

Make a Peanut Lamb

This lamb can remind you to have faith that Jesus offered Himself as a sacrifice to take away your sins.

What You Need

- 2 peanuts (one with 2 nuts inside, one with 1 nut inside, see illustration)
- black pipe cleaner (chenille wire)
- scissors
- glue
- cotton balls
- black marker
- typing correction fluid or white paint

What You Do

1. *Use the marker to color the face part of the small peanut. Dot correction fluid or paint on the face for eyes.*
2. *Cut the pipe cleaner into pieces that will be the lamb's 2 ears, neck, 4 legs, and tail.*
3. *Poke holes in the peanuts where the pipe cleaners will be. Bend the pipe cleaners to look like legs, ears, a neck, and a tail. Glue the pipe cleaners in the holes.*
4. *Glue on pieces of cotton balls to look like the picture.*
5. *Put your lamb where you can see it. Remember how much God loves you whenever you look at it!*

Draw a star in this box when you've read John 1:29; Hebrews 9:7, 11-14.

A House on a Rock

Ask Jesus to be your Lord. Live your life by what He says in the Bible and by what you learn when you pray, then you'll be building your "house" on a "rock"!

Can you draw this house without lifting your pencil and without redrawing any of the lines?

Draw Here

When you can draw this house without lifting your pencil, dip a single piece of twine in glue and glue it to a rock in the shape of a house. Write "Jesus is my Lord, and I will obey Him." on the rock with a permanent marker.

The Mediator

Have you ever had two friends who had a problem come between them? If you helped them work it out and get back together, you were a mediator. Sin has come between God and us. Jesus is the mediator who gets us back together with God.

Before Adam and Eve disobeyed God, they walked with God in the Garden of Eden. But then they disobeyed and sin entered the world and got between God and us. Jesus came to get sin out of the way so we could be with God. You can see how this works by using pepper, soap, and matches in a bowl of water.

Show How Jesus Gets Rid of Sin

What You Need

- help from an adult to use matches
- burned-out matches
- plastic knife
- Ivory soap
- pen
- two 3" x 5" index cards
- tape
- bowl
- shaker of black pepper
- red tissue or construction paper

How You Prepare

1. *Use a plastic knife to carve a scrap of Ivory soap (it floats) into a cross.*
2. *Write "GOD" on an index card. Tape it inside a bowl so that most of the card sticks up outside of the bowl (see the picture).*
3. *Fill the bowl with water.*
4. *Write "SIN" on half of an index card and tape it to a can or shaker of black pepper.*
5. *Ask a grown-up to burn the tips of 2 matches and dip them in water so they're safe for you. DO NOT light the matches yourself!*
6. *Tape a piece of red paper shaped like a flame to one of the matches. It represents a "NEW PERSON." The other burned-out match represents a "SINFUL PERSON."*

What You Do

You can show your family and friends how Jesus gets rid of our sin.

1. *Sin separates people from God. (Sprinkle pepper between the "GOD" card and "SINFUL PERSON" match.)*
2. *When a person trusts Jesus as the only way to be saved, that person is born again and can be "on fire" for God. (Throw away burned-out "SINFUL PERSON" match. Put "NEW PERSON" match on cross.)*
3. *Jesus gets rid of sin that separates us from God. (Place cross in water and pepper will quickly float away from it.)*
4. *Jesus takes us to God. (Blow on cross until it floats over to the "GOD" card.)*

Draw a star in this box when you've read Romans 5:11, 18; and I Timothy 2:5.

The Messiah

Do you remember what the Greek name "Christ" means? "Messiah" is a Hebrew name that means the same thing. *To find the meaning in the puzzle, start with the "A," skip the next letter, and write the letter after that. Continue around the drop of oil. When you get back to the A, write the letter following it and continue around the drop again. When you are finished, you will have the meaning of the name Messiah.*

Jesus Fulfilled the Prophecies

The Jewish people were waiting for the Messiah to come. They had lots of descriptions of what He would be like from the prophecies of the Old Testament. (A prophecy is often a message from God that tells about something that will happen in the future.) Every one of those prophecies were true of Jesus. Some of them were about when He came to earth the first time, and some were about when He will come back, but they were all about Him. *Unscramble some of them.*

Prophecy: Micah 5:2
Fulfilled: Matthew 2:1-6

1. Born in HETBELMEH.

Prophecy: Zechariah 9:9
Fulfilled: Matthew 21:1-9

2. Rode into Jerusalem on a NEKYOD.

Prophecy: Psalm 22:16-18
Fulfilled: Matthew 27:35

3. Died on a SRSOC.

Prophecy: Isaiah 53:12
Fulfilled: Matthew 27:38

4. Suffered with BORREBS.

Prophecy: Psalm 69:21
Fulfilled: Mark 15:36

5. Offered a drink of GARVINE.

Prophecy: Psalm 16:10
Fulfilled: Matthew 28:5, 6

6. Raised from the EDAD.

☐ *Draw a star in this box when you've read each of the prophecies and fulfillments listed on this page.*

The Great Physician

Jesus is called the Great Physician because He makes people well. Can you fill in the blanks? You can find the answers in the Bible verses.

1. This man's friends lowered him through the roof to get him to Jesus. Jesus made him able to walk. What else did Jesus do for him?

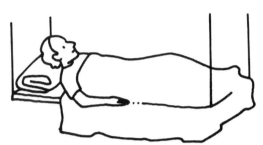

F _ _ _ _ _ _ _   _ _ _   _ _ _ S   (Luke 5:17-25)

2. Who were three dead people Jesus brought back to life?

L _ _ _ _ _ S (John 11: 38-44)

The S _ _ of a _ _ _ _ W (Luke 7:11-15)

The D _ _ _ _ _ _ _ of _ _ _ _ _ S (Mark 5:21-24, 35-43)

3. Jesus healed the blind eyes of a beggar named

B _ _ _ _ _ _ _ _ S. (Mark 10:46-52)

4. Jesus healed Peter's mother-in-law, who had a

F _ _ _ R. (Matthew 8:14, 15)

5. When Jesus healed 10 lepers, only one came back to

T _ _ _ _   _ _ M. (Luke 17:11-19)

Draw a star in this box when you've read Matthew 8:14, 15; 9:1-8; Mark 5:21-23; 5:35-43; 10:46-52; Luke 7:11-18; 17:11-19; John 11:1-53.

The Redeemer

People once bought and sold other people. A slave was a person whom someone else owned, and who had to do whatever the owner said. Often a slave's only ticket to freedom was if he could find a redeemer. A redeemer was someone who bought a slave to set him free. The payment was called a ransom.

Sin makes people slaves; they aren't free to do what will really make them happy. They keep doing wrong things that make their lives hard and miserable. But Jesus paid his blood as a ransom to free people from sin. When people believe the truth about Jesus, they are set free.

Make a Ransom Note

A kidnapper is someone who takes a person away from those who love him. The kidnapper sometimes writes a "ransom note" asking for money to let that person go. The kidnapped person is not freed until someone who loves him pays the price (the ransom).

You can make your own ransom note. Just cut out letters and words from old magazines and newspapers to spell the message on this ransom note. Paste them onto this page.

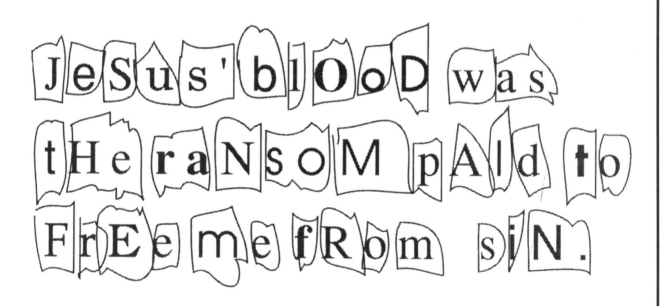

Draw a star in this box when you've read Matthew 20:28; Mark 10:45; John 8:31, 32, 34, 36; I Timothy 2:6.

The Resurrection and the Life

Jesus said, "I am the resurrection and the life. He who believes in me will live, even though he dies; and whoever lives and believes in me will never die."

The word "resurrect" means to raise from the dead. Because of Jesus, we will be raised from the dead after our bodies die. The life He gives us when we believe in Him is eternal—it will never end. Because Jesus died on the cross for you, your spirit can live with Him in heaven forever.

Decode this puzzle. In the blank below each picture, write the first letter of the word that begins the picture.

_ _ _ _ _   _ _ _ _   _ _ _ _ _

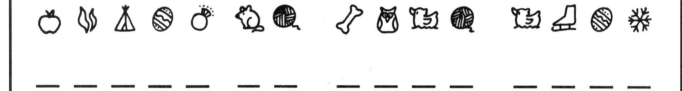

_ _ _ _ _ _ _   _ _ _ _   _ _ _ _

_ _ _ _ _ _ _   _ _   _ _ _ _ _ .

☐ *Draw a star in this box when you've read John 11:25, 26.*

The Rock

Find and circle the letters of JESUS on the rock. Find and circle the letters of HOLY SPIRIT in the water.

In Old Testament times Moses and the Israelites came to a place in the desert where there wasn't anything to drink, so God gave them water out of a rock. That rock was like Jesus.

Jesus told a woman at a well, "Whoever drinks the water I give him will never thirst. Indeed, the water I give him will become in him a spring of water welling up to eternal life."

Jesus also said at another time, "If anyone is thirsty, let him come to me and drink. Whoever believes in me, as the Scripture has said, streams of living water will flow from within him." The living water that Jesus was talking about is the Holy Spirit. People who believe in Jesus receive the Holy Spirit.

Have you ever been terribly thirsty? Just like our bodies get thirsty for water, our spirits get thirsty for God. When you come to Jesus, the Rock, and believe in Him as your Savior, He will fill you with the living water of the Holy Spirit.

Draw a star in this box when you've read John 4:13, 14; 7:37-39; and I Corinthians 10:4.

The Savior

When a person is in major trouble, it is sometimes called being in "deep water." Sin is the deepest water we can get into, but putting your faith in Jesus is like taking hold of a lifesaver that can pull you out of danger.

Take Hold of the Lifesaver

A gift is not something that you earn. It is given free of charge. Salvation is a gift from God, and He wants you to accept it like you would accept any present—just take it. The life preserver is being held out to you and all you have to do is hold onto it. There is only one name on the life preserver that can save you. The name that saves is Jesus.

To be saved, believe that Jesus is the Son of God, that He died to take the punishment for your sins, and that He lives again. Trust Him as the only way for you to get to heaven, and promise to follow Him as your Lord.

To Accept Jesus as Your Savior and Lord, Pray a Prayer Like This in Your Own Words:

Dear God,

I love You. I know that I don't deserve to live with You because of anything I have done, but I am thankful that You offer eternal life to me as a free gift because of Your Son, Jesus. I believe He is who He said He was. Please forgive my sins because He died for me. I am putting my trust in Him as my Savior and I will follow Him as my Lord all of my life. Thank You for saving me.

In Jesus' name I pray. Amen.

Make a Lifesaver Pendant

To let others know how glad you are that Jesus saved you, you can make this pendant. When people notice you wearing it, explain to them how Jesus is your lifesaver. If they want to be saved, too, help them pray a prayer like the one on this page.

Draw a star in this box when you've read Matthew 10:22; 24:13; Acts 4:12; Romans 10:9, 10, 13; and Ephesians 2:8.

Servant

After the Last Supper, Jesus washed each of the disciples' feet to show that He was willing to serve them. He said, "The greatest among you should be like the youngest, and the one who rules like the one who serves. For who is greater, the one who is at the table or the one who serves? Is it not the one who is at the table? But I am among you as one who serves." Jesus served us, and He wants us to serve each other.

Serve Your Family

Trace the right foot of each member of your family on colored paper. Cut out the paper feet and glue them onto a sheet of white paper. List things on each foot that you can do for that foot's owner this week.

If the rest of the family wants to get involved, make a foot picture for each of them to write on, too.

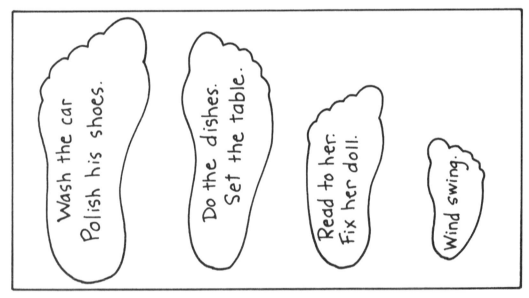

Draw a star in this box when you've read Luke 22:26, 27; and John 13:4-15.

The Good Shepherd

Jesus said, "I am the good shepherd; I know my sheep and my sheep know me—just as the Father knows me and I know the Father—and I lay down my life for the sheep. I have other sheep that are not of this sheep pen. I must bring them also. They too will listen to my voice, and there shall be one flock and one shepherd."

Jesus also said, "My sheep listen to my voice; I know them, and they follow me. I give them eternal life, and they shall never perish; no one can snatch them out of my hand. My Father, who has given them to me, is greater than all; no one can snatch them out of my Father's hand. I and the Father are one."

Make a Gumdrop Lamb and Shepherd

Use these candies to remind you to follow the Good Shepherd!

What You Need

- 10 gumdrops (4 white, 2 black, 2 pairs of any color)
- 9 toothpicks
- scissors
- food coloring

What You Do to Make the Shepherd

1. *Cut four toothpicks in half with scissors. Don't break them; that could leave splinters.*
2. *Make a body by connecting two colored gumdrops with a toothpick half.*
3. *Use another toothpick half to stick a white gumdrop to the body for a head.*
4. *Stick a toothpick half on each side of the body for arms. Pinch two pieces off of a white gumdrop and stick one onto each arm for hands. Stick a whole toothpick through one of the hands for a shepherd's staff.*
5. *Stick two toothpick halves into the gumdrop body for legs, and stick a colored gumdrop at the end of each leg for feet. Adjust the toothpicks and gumdrops until the shepherd can stand.*
6. *Dip the tip of a whole toothpick in a drop of food coloring. Draw a face on the head. Let dry.*

What You Do to Make the Lamb

1. *Cut four toothpicks in half with scissors. Don't break them; that could leave splinters.*
2. *Connect two white gumdrops with a toothpick half to make a body.*
3. *Use a toothpick half to connect a black gumdrop to the body for a head.*
4. *Pinch a small piece off of a black gumdrop and attach it to the body with a toothpick half for a tail.*
5. *Stick four toothpick halves into the body for legs and adjust them until your sheep will stand.*

Draw a star in this box when you've read John 10:14-16, 27-30.

The Son of God

Jesus' Father was God. When Jesus was baptized, God spoke from heaven and said, "This is my Son, whom I love; with him I am well pleased." Another time when God spoke from heaven about Jesus is called "The Transfiguration." Think about how you would have felt if you were there.

The Transfiguration

Change each BOLD, CAPITALIZED word to its opposite, and read this story.

One (1) **NIGHT** _____ Jesus took Peter, James, and John with Him (2) **DOWN** _____ a mountain to pray. As Jesus prayed, He started to look different. His face shone like the (3) **MOON** _____, and His clothes became as (4) **BLACK** _____ as light. Moses and Elijah, prophets from (5) **NEW** _____ Testament times, (6) **DISAPPEARED** _____ and talked with Jesus about his upcoming (7) **BIRTH** _____ in Jerusalem.

Peter said, "It is (8) **BAD** _____ for us to be (9) **THERE** _____. Let us put up three shelters—one for you, one for Moses, and one for Elijah." While (10) **SHE** _____ was talking, a (11) **DIM** _____ cloud covered them and a voice from the cloud said, "This is my Son whom I have chosen; listen to Him!"

Peter, James, and John fell flat (12) **OFF** _____ their faces and were terrified. Jesus came to them, touched them, and said, "Get up, and don't be afraid." When they looked (13) **DOWN** _____, they only saw Jesus. He was standing by Himself.

☐ *Draw a star in this box when you've read Matthew 3:17; 17:1-8; Mark 1:11; 9:2-8; Luke 9:28-36.*

The True Vine

Fill in each blank with the word from the grape that has the same number. Then read what Jesus said about being the true vine.

___ ___ ___ ___ ; ___ ___ ___
 1   2   3   4   5   6   7

___ ___ ___ ___ ___ ___ .
      8   9 10 11   12

___ ___ ___ ___ ___ ___ , ___
13 14 15 16 17 18   19

___ ___ ___ ___ ;
20   21   22   23

___ ___ ___ ___
24   25   26   27

___ ___ .
28   29

___ ___
30   31

___ ___ ___
32   33   34

___ ___ .
35   36

___ ___
37   38

___ ___
39   40

___ .
41

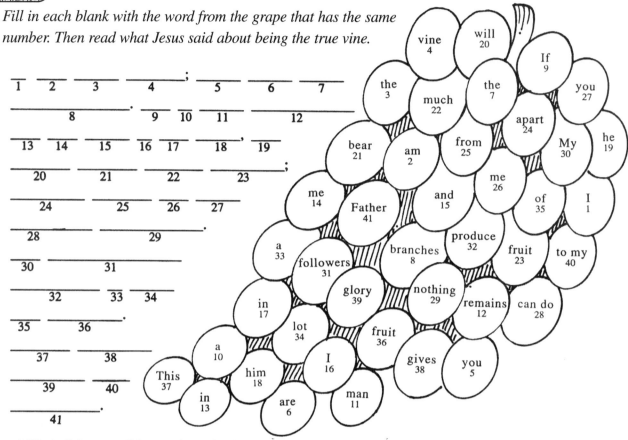

Good "fruits" in your life are the attitudes and actions God wants you to have. If you have accepted Jesus, He is like a vine that feeds you and gives you everything you need to be who God wants you to be and do what God wants you to do.

When you produce good fruit, it glorifies God and shows that you are Jesus' follower. You are only able to do the good that Jesus wants you to do if you stay close to Him—branches can't grow grapes if they are pulled off the vine!

Bear Good Fruit

Pray and ask God what He would like you to do. Listen carefully and then write some of those things on these grapes. Ask the Lord to help you do the things that He wants you to do.

Your Attitudes & Actions: The Grapes

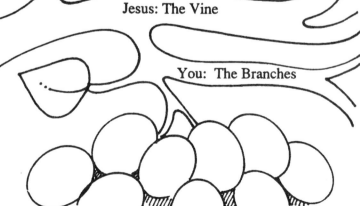

Jesus: The Vine

You: The Branches

☐ *Draw a star in this box when you've read John 15:5, 8.*

The Way

Jesus said, "I am the way and the truth and the life. No one comes to the Father except through me." You can't save yourself by doing good. Your church can't save you. Not even your parents can save you. Jesus is the only way to get to heaven. The Bible says, "it is by grace you have been saved, through faith—and this not from yourselves, it is the gift of God—not by works, so that no one can boast." Eternal life in Jesus is a free gift. All you have to do is accept it!

Make a Ladder That Shows the Way to God

What You Need

- drinking straws (two complete straws and four 2 1/2-inch pieces cut from straws)
- hole punch or scissors
- paper towel
- glue
- alphabet macaroni

What You Do

1. *Punch or cut four holes about an inch apart through both sides of a straw. Make sure that the holes are directly across from each other. Repeat with another straw.*

2. *Poke the straw pieces through the holes to make a ladder.*

3. *Lay the ladder on the paper towel and glue on alphabet letters that spell "Faith in Jesus is the only way."*

Draw a star in this box when you've read John 14:6; and Ephesians 2:8, 9.

The Word

People use words to let others know what they are thinking. Jesus let us know what God thinks, so Jesus is called "The Word."

A Word Puzzle

There are some words from John 1:1-3 hidden in this puzzle. The words can go up and down, left and right, or diagonally.

Look for these words: WORD, BEGINNING, WERE, ALL, GOD, THINGS, MADE, HIM

```
S  G  N  I  H  T  J  L  F
L  N  Z  O  P  Q  L  P  N
T  I  K  W  E  A  H  Y  R
F  N  S  E  O  M  G  I  M
J  N  M  L  L  R  O  E  A
Y  I  I  R  A  M  D  A  D
E  G  H  A  B  W  R  T  E
D  E  L  A  W  E  R  E  A
M  B  E  N  A  N  D  I  L
```

Decide if the sentences below are true or false. Circle the letter under the correct answer for each sentence. If your answers are right, they will spell a word. (You can check your answers in John 1:1-3.)

	True	False
1. Jesus wasn't with God in the beginning.	R	W
2. Jesus was God.	O	A
3. Everything was made through Jesus.	R	K
4. Some things were made without Jesus.	L	D

☐ *Draw a star in this box when you've read John 1:1-3.*

I Did It!

COMPLETED	DATE	COMPLETED	DATE
☐ Seek and You Will Find	_____	☐ The Light	_____
☐ Add a Line	_____	☐ The Lord	_____
☐ Alpha and Omega	_____	☐ The Mediator	_____
☐ The Bread of Life	_____	☐ The Messiah	_____
☐ The Bridegroom	_____	☐ The Great Physician	_____
☐ The Christ	_____	☐ The Redeemer	_____
☐ Commander	_____	☐ The Resurrection and the Life	_____
☐ The Chief Cornerstone	_____	☐ The Rock	_____
☐ Friend	_____	☐ The Savior	_____
☐ The Gate	_____	☐ Servant	_____
☐ Gift of God	_____	☐ The Good Shepherd	_____
☐ God	_____	☐ The Son of God	_____
☐ Immanuel	_____	☐ The True Vine	_____
☐ Jesus	_____	☐ The Way	_____
☐ The King of Kings	_____	☐ The Word	_____
☐ The Lamb of God	_____		

Following Jesus

The Work God Wants

In John 6:28, 29 some people asked Jesus, "What does God want us to do?" These people thought they could gain eternal life by good works. *Decode Jesus' answer to discover the "works" God wants. Below each cross, write the letter that has the same pattern as the cross.*

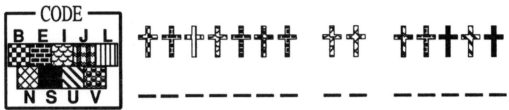

Keep the Faith

How long does Jesus want us to keep believing in Him? *Fill in the blanks with letters to find what Jesus said in Matthew 10:22 and Mark 13:13. Begin with the letter H at the to of the cross. Write that letter, then skip a letter as you go around the cross. The second time you go around the cross, begin with the letter T that follows the letter H.*

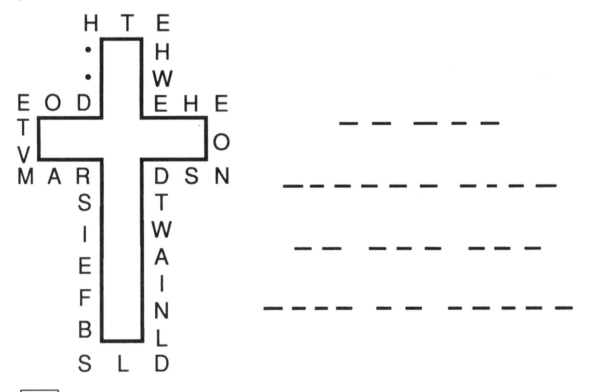

Draw a star in this box when you've read Matthew 10:22; Mark 13:13; and John 6:28, 29.

Love with all Your Heart

Someone once asked Jesus which commandment was the most important. Jesus said to love God will all your heart, soul, mind, and strength. He also said that the second greatest commandment is to love your neighbor as yourself. You can show your love for God as you love others. *Write the names of people you know in these hearts, one name per heart.*

Each day do the following for one of these people:

• *Pray and ask the Lord to take care of the needs that person has. Also ask God to show you what you can do for that person. If he or she doesn't know the Lord, ask God to help you find a good time to talk to the person about Him.*

• *Do kind things for that person, but don't let anyone know about it.*

• *When you find a good time to talk about God, ask that person if he or she has ever trusted Jesus as Savior. If necessary, you can use page 14 to explain how to become a Christian.*

Draw a star in this box when you've read Matthew 22:35-40 and Mark 12:28-34.

Be Born Again

Nicodemus Visits Jesus

In John 3:1-21, a Pharisee named Nicodemus came to Jesus. *Read about his nighttime visit with Jesus and color the pictures.*

Everyone was born once. For our physical bodies that's enough, but God wants each of us to be born again. The second time is when we are born into the family of God and become a new person on the inside. The second birth happens when we trust Jesus to save us from our sins. You can be born again right now. If you'd like, pray a prayer like this in your own words:

Dear God, I want to be born again. I believe Jesus is Your Son and that He died for me so I could be forgiven and could live with You. Please make me the way You want me to be. I'll follow Jesus all of my life. In Jesus' name I pray. Amen.

Draw a star in this box when you've read John 1:12; 3:1-21; II Corinthians 5:17 and Galatians 3:26.

My Birth Announcements

When you were born, your parents probably sent out birth announcements to tell all their friends the good news of your birth! You can fill in the following birth announcements. One for the first time you were born, and the second for when you choose to be born again.

First, fill in the birth announcement of your first birth. If you prayed the prayer on page 51 for the first time today, you are born again. Write today's date on the rebirth announcement. If you have already asked Jesus to be your Lord and Savior, write the day you did that on the rebirth announcement. If you don't remember the day, that's okay–God knows!

Punch holes where there are circles in the cards, and stick paper reinforcements over the holes. Thread pink or blue ribbons through the holes and tie a bow on each announcement.

Draw a star in this box when you've read John 3:1-9; II Corinthians 5:17; Galatians 3:26; and John 1:12.

Join the Family

Hebrews 11:6 says that you can't please God without faith. When you have faith in Jesus, He helps you do what God wants you to do. When you do God's will, it shows that you have trusted Jesus and are following Him.

One day while Jesus was talking to a crowd, His mother and brothers wanted to speak to Him. When someone told Jesus, He pointed to His followers and said that people who hear God's Word and do it are His family.

A Family Portrait

If you trust Jesus as your Savior and you try to follow Him, draw yourself in this family portrait. Ask your friends or family if they have trusted Jesus as their Savior. If they have, ask them to draw themselves in the picture. If they're not sure, explain how someone can become a member of God's family.

Another time when Jesus was teaching, a woman in the crowd called out, "Your mother is blessed." Jesus said that those who hear the word of God and obey it are blessed (Luke 11:27, 28).

On a separate sheet of paper, write a few things you know God wants you to do. After you do each thing, write beside it how you were blessed by it. For example:

What God would like me to do:

Write to Grandma.

Tell Pam I was sorry.

Tell John about Jesus.

How I was blessed:

She said my letter made her happy.

She forgave me.

I felt great when he became a Christian.

Draw a star in this box when you've read Matthew 12:46-50; Luke 8:19-21; 11:27, 28; Hebrews 11:6.

Get on the Narrow Road

When you learn that Jesus can save you, it is like coming to the gate of a road that leads to life forever with God. You can choose whether to get on this road or another. Find what Jesus said about this in Matthew 7:13, 14. *Fill in the missing words and then fit them into the puzzle.*

____ ____ ____ ____ ____ through the narrow ____ ____ ____ ____. For wide is the gate and broad is the road that leads to destruction, and many enter through it. But small is the gate and ___ ___ ___ ___ ___ ___ the road that leads to ___ ___ ___ ___ , and only a ___ ___ ___ find it.

Draw a star in this box when you've read Matthew 7:13, 14.

The Old and the New

Jesus told a parable about wine and patches. In New Testament times, people poured wine into wineskins. If they put new wine into an old dry wineskin, it would explode. New wine had to go into new wineskins.

If you got a new pair of jeans, would you cut a piece out of them to patch an old pair? Why not?

What would be wrong with the new pair?
What would be wrong with the old pair?

A Patchwork Puzzle

Each piece of fabric in this quilt has words needed to discover what Jesus was telling people when He talked about wine and patches. Write the word or words in the blank above the correct number.

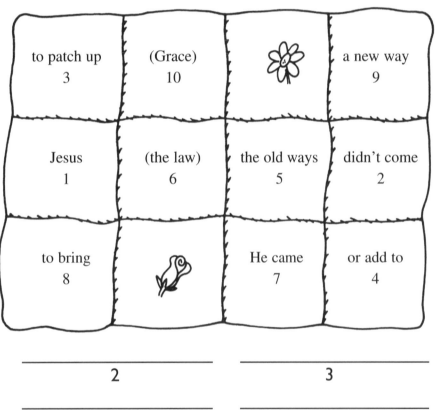

to patch up 3	(Grace) 10	✿	a new way 9
Jesus 1	(the law) 6	the old ways 5	didn't come 2
to bring 8	🌹	He came 7	or add to 4

_____ _____ _____
   1   2   3

_____ _____ _____
   4   5   6

_____ _____ _____
   7   8   9   10

☐ *Draw a star in this box when you've read Matthew 9:16, 17; Mark 2:21, 22; Luke 5:36-39.*

Build Your House on the Rock

In Luke 6:46-49, Jesus told a story to show people what a person is like who hears God's Word and practices it. Jesus said, "Whoever comes to Me, hears the things I say and does them will be like a man building a house who dug deep and built the house on a rock. When it stormed and a flood came, the house stood firm because it was well built. But whoever hears and doesn't do what I say is like a man who built his house on the ground without a foundation. The moment the floods came, the house fell and was ruined."

Build a House on the Rock

When you trust Jesus and plan your life on what He says in the Bible, you'll be building your "house" on the "rock."

What You Need

- empty 1/2-gallon milk carton
- scissors
- stapler
- colored paper or fabric
- tape
- tacky glue
- markers
- large, flat rock
- blank piece of paper

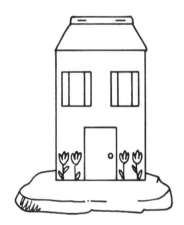
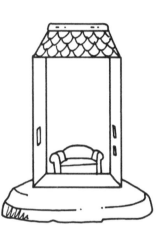

What You Do

1. *Rinse out the milk carton, staple the top shut, and cut away one side.*
2. *Decorate the outside to look like a house. Cover it with colored paper. Draw on it with markers.*
3. *Decorate the inside to look like a house. Glue a carpet scrap or piece of fabric onto the "floor." Cover the "walls" with wallpaper scraps or colored paper. Make miniature furniture from match boxes, pill bottles, and other small objects or glue on pictures of furniture cut from old catalogs. Decorate the "walls" with miniature paintings you've made and a "mirror" cut from foil. Cut out the windows.*
4. *Write on the roof "My Life." Write on the rock "What Jesus says."*
5. *Glue the house onto the rock.*
6. *On a piece of paper, list some of the things you want Jesus to decide in your life and glue this list inside the house.*

☐ *Draw a star in this box when you've read Luke 6:46-49.*

Love Each Other

Show You Follow Jesus by Showing Love

Jesus said, "A new command I give you: Love one another. As I have loved you, so you must love one another. By this all men will know that you are my disciples [followers], if you love one another." *Make a card to express your love for others.*

Make an Embossed Card

What You Need

- poster board
- pencil
- sheet of typing paper
- sheet of construction paper
- scissors
- tape

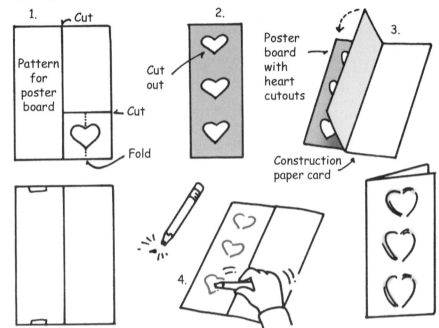

What You Do

1. *Fold the typing paper in half lengthwise as shown. Cut along the fold and use half as a pattern to cut a piece of poster board. Cut a heart out of the other half of the sheet of typing paper.*
2. *Trace three hearts on the poster board piece. Cut the hearts out of the poster board piece.*
3. *Fold the piece of construction paper in half lengthwise. Lay the left side on top of the piece of poster board that has hearts cut out of it. Tape them together.*
4. *You'll need to break the lead out of your pencil by pressing it against a scrap piece of paper on a table. Use the pencil without lead to rub across the construction paper until the paper is pressed into the heart cutouts.*
5. *Very carefully remove the tape.*
6. *Write a letter inside the construction paper card. It should fit inside a business envelope.*

☐ *Draw a star in this box when you've read John 13:34, 35; 15:17.*

Tell the Good News

There's good news and bad news. First, the bad news: everyone sins and that makes us unable to live with God. Now for the good news: God takes our sins away so we can live with Him if we have faith that Jesus died for our sins and was resurrected. Those of us who are forgiven are very thankful to God. Think how glad other people will be when they know that Jesus loves them and will forgive them! He says people are like grain (such as wheat) that is ripe and ready to be harvested (gathered). We should help bring these people to Jesus. We should also pray for God to send more workers to help with the harvest.

Using the words at the bottom of this newspaper, fill in the blanks to complete the Bad News and Good News.

Bad News

_____ of us deserve to _____ with God because we have all _____.

Good News

If we have _____ in _____, our _____ are _____ and we will live with God.

Word Bank:
sinned, Jesus, None, sins, forgiven, live, faith

Draw a star in this box when you've read John 4:35-38; Matthew 9:37, 38; Romans 3:23; 5:1, 2.

Make a T-Shirt to Help with the Harvest

Wear this T-shirt that announces the good news you have to tell about Jesus. When people ask about your shirt, first explain the bad news, and then tell them the good news. If they want to trust Jesus, offer to pray with them.

What You Need

- pre-washed T-shirt
- cardboard
- pencil
- fabric paint pens

What You Do

1. *Put the cardboard inside the shirt to prevent paint from soaking through the front of the shirt and onto the back.*

2. *Write "I Have Good News" with pencil on the shirt.*

3. *Trace over the pencil letters with fabric paint pens. If you make mistakes, let them dry. Then trace around each letter with a different color to cover the mistakes.*

4. *Decorate the shirt however you like.*

5. *Let the shirt dry before wearing it.*

Jesus' Overpaid Workers

Fill in the blanks and read this story Jesus told about workers in the kingdom of God.

The __ ingdom of heaven i__ like a landowner wh__
18   4   2
hired some people to work in his vineyard early one morning. They agreed to be paid a coin called a denarius for
the d__y and we__t to work. At different times throughout
6   13
the ___ay, the landowner hired more workers. He told
3
these workers he would pay them whate__er was right.
15

In the evenin__ it __as time to pay the work__rs.
1   17   8
__he people hired __ast were paid first. Eve__yone
11   16   5

Find a Message

*Find a message the story teaches by putting the letters that are missing
from the numbered blanks of the story into these numbered blanks.*

___ ___ ___ , ___   ___ ___ ___ ___   ___ ___
1   2   3   4   1   5   6   7   8   9   4

___ ___ ___ ___   ___ ___ ___ ___   ___ ___ ___ ___ ___ ___
10 2   5   8   11 12 6   13   6   13 14 2   13 8

___ ___ ___ ___ ___ ___ ___ ___ , ___ ___ ___   ___ ___
3   8   4   8   5   15 8   4   6   13 3   12 8

___ ___ ___ ___ ___   ___ ___   ___ ___ ___   ___ ___ ___ ___
1   9   15 8   4   9   11   11 12 8   4   6   10 8

___ ___   ___ ___ ___   ___ ___ ___   ___ ___ ___ ___ ___
11 2   6   16 16   17 12 2   8   13 11 8   5

___ ___ ___   ___ ___ ___ ___ ___ ___ ___ .
12 9   4   18 9   13 1   3   2   10

received a denarius __₇*oin. The ones who worked
longest thought they should have been paid more.*

*The landowner said, "I'm being fair to you. Didn't you
agree to work for a denarius? Take your pay and go. I
want to pa*__₁₄ *the many I hired the same amount* __₉ *gave
you. Don't I have the right to do what I want wit*__₁₂ *my
own* __₁₀*oney? Are you envious because I am generous?*

☐ *Draw a star in this box when you've read Matthew 20:1-16.*

Let Your Light Shine

In Matthew 5:14-16, Jesus said, "You are the light of the world. A city on a hill cannot be hidden. Neither do people light a lamp and put it under a bowl. Instead they put it on its stand, and it gives light to everyone in the house. In the same way, let your light shine before men, that they may see your good deeds and praise your Father in heaven."

A Bright Idea Puzzle

Find each picture's word in the puzzle and color those letters yellow. Fill in the remaining letters with a black pen to find a bright idea.

STARBRIGHTENLAMP
TORCHTHESUNWORLD
AROUNDFLASHLIGHT
LIGHTBULBYOULANTERN
BYCANDLELETTINGCAMPFIRE
PEOPLELIGHTNINGSEE
JESUSLIGHTHOUSEIN
FIREWORKSYOU

Draw a star in this box when you've read Matthew 5:14-16.

A Bright Reminder

You can let your light shine for Jesus wherever you are. *Make this candleholder to remind you to shine brightly for Jesus.*

What You Need

- a clean jar (baby food jars work well)
- ruler
- construction paper
- scissors
- tape
- pencil
- pushpin
- newspaper
- a votive candle or other small candle

I WILL LET MY LIGHT SHINE

What You Do

1. *Measure the width and height of the jar. Cut a strip of construction paper that will cover the jar.*
2. *Write "I will let my light shine" in simple letters on the construction paper strip. Lay it on newspaper.*
3. *Poke evenly spaced holes in the letters.*
4. *Tape the strip around the OUTSIDE of the jar.*
5. *Place the candle inside the jar.*
6. *When you burn the candle, remember to let Jesus' light shine in you.*

Unscramble these ways to let your light shine.

VIEG A GIB LIMES

_____

LETL TOBUA SEUJS

_____

FEOFR OT PHLE OPELPE

_____

OFGREIV TOHRES

_____

A City on a Hill

Find a postcard of a big city. Use a straight pin to poke holes where there are windows in buildings. Hold a flashlight behind the postcard in the dark to see what the city would look like at night.

Be Salty

In Matthew 5:13, Jesus said, "You are the salt of the earth. But if the salt loses its saltiness, how can it be made salty again? It is no longer good for anything, except to be thrown out and trampled by men."

Serve salted and unsalted popcorn to your family or friends. Can they tell a difference? Jesus doesn't want you to just blend in with everyone else in the world. He wants you to make a noticeable difference like salt makes a noticeable difference in food. If you tell people they can be saved through faith in Jesus, that makes their lives better the way salt makes food taste better.

Salt Picture

Make a colored salt picture to remind you that Jesus wants His followers to be the salt of the earth—and make a difference for Him.

What You Need

- salt
- paper cups
- food coloring
- paper plate
- pencil
- newspaper
- glue

To make colored salt: You'll need one paper cup for each color. Fill each paper cup about 1/4 full of salt. Add one drop of food coloring. Stir well.

What You Do

1. Draw your face on a paper plate and write "I am the salt of the earth" beneath it.

2. Trace a section of the picture lightly with glue and sprinkle on colored salt. Shake off the extra colored salt onto a piece of newspaper. Add more glue and colored salt until the plate is covered.

Draw a star in this box when you've read Matthew 5:13; Mark 9:50; Luke 14:34.

The Prodigal Son

In Luke 15:11-24, Jesus told a great parable that some people call "The Prodigal Son." The parable goes like this. A man had two sons. One day the younger son asked his father for the money he was supposed to get after his father died. The father gave the money to him.

Soon after that the younger son left home with everything he had and went far away. The son wasted his money and when it was all gone, he needed to find a job. The only work he could get was feeding pigs for a farmer. He was so poor and hungry that even the pigs' food looked good to him. He thought, "Why am I starving when my father's servants have plenty to eat? Even though I don't deserve to be called his son anymore, I'm going home and will beg my father to let me work for him."

When the father saw the son coming, he ran to welcome his son. The father kissed him, hugged him, and gave him clothes. Then the father had his servants prepare a special dinner to celebrate the return of his son.

Sometimes we're like the son in the story. We run away from God and do things our own way. Even though we long to go back to God, we're afraid He will be angry. God is like the father in the story. He will welcome us back and forgive us. That's how much God loves us.

Help the Son Get Back to His Father

Draw a star in this box when you've read Luke 15:11-24.

Help the Poor

In Luke 16:19-31, Jesus told a story to warn the wealthy about being selfish and trusting their wealth instead of Him.

Read the story and complete the puzzle with the missing words.

A rich man wore fancy _____ (5-down) and lived in luxury every day. A poor _____ (3-down) named Lazarus laid at the rich man's gate longing to eat the scraps that fell from the rich man's _____ (6-across). Lazarus was covered with sores, which the dogs licked.

Both men _____ (4-across). The angels carried Lazarus to be with the prophet Abraham. The rich man was buried and went to hell. While he was suffering there, he saw Abraham and Lazarus far way. He called out to say to Abraham, "Feel sorry for me. Send Lazarus to dip the tip of his finger in _____ (2-across) and cool my tongue, because I am in agony in this fire."

Abraham said, "Remember that in your lifetime you received good things while Lazarus received bad things, but now he is comforted here and you are in agony. Also, a big hole has been made between us so no one can go from here to there or from there to here."

The man who had been rich said, "Then please send Lazarus to _____ (2-down) my five brothers so they won't also come to this place of torment."

Abraham said, "They have the words of the _____ (7-across) [in the Bible]. If they won't listen [to what is in the Bible], they won't believe even if someone rose from the _____ (1-down)."

Draw a star in this box when you've read Luke 16:19-31.

Make Clothespin Puppets

*Use these clothespin puppets to act out the story
Jesus told about Lazarus and the rich man.*

What You Need

- 3 clothespins
- markers
- small pieces of colorful fabrics
- small pieces of brown fabric
- small pieces of white fabric
- twine
- glue
- scissors

What You Do

1. *Using the markers, draw a face on each of the three clothespins.*

2. *Cut out a piece of colorful fabric and wrap around one of the clothespin puppets. Tie twine around the middle for a belt. This is the rich man.*

3. *Cut out a piece of brown fabric, wrap around one of the clothespins, and tie in the middle with a piece of twine. This is Lazarus.*

4. *Cut out a piece of white fabric, wrap around the last of the clothespins, and tie a piece of twine around the middle. This is Abraham.*

5. *Pieces of fabric can be cut out and glued to the heads of the puppets if you'd like.*

6. *Act out the story of the rich man and Lazarus.*

The Rich Young Man

Figure out this word picture puzzle to read about the conversation Jesus had with a rich young man.

A +thy young had tried all of his life 2 do what was .

When he asked how he could have eternal life, said 4 him 2

sell everything he owned, 2 give the $ 2 the poor, & 2 follow . The

young went away   + cause he was very +thy.

 said, "It is easier 4 a 2 through the 👁 (hole) of A

than 4 A +thy 2 N + 2 the +dom of God."

Find the Promise

Color the shapes that do not have dollar or cent signs in them.

If you agree with the promise, sign your name here.

Signed, _____

☐ *Draw a star in this box when you've read Matthew 19:16-26; Mark 10:17-27; Luke 18:18-27.*

Choose Your Master

Even though you don't have a job yet, it's important to decide now whether you'll spend your life trying to get rich or trying to follow God. In Matthew 6:24 and Luke 16:13-15, Jesus said you can't do both. You have to make a choice.

Who Will Be Your Master?

Circle one.

Use this code to find out what Jesus said.

A = ①

G = ㉕

O =

D = ⑤

M =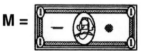

Y =

E = ⑩

N =

"YOU CANNOT SERVE BOTH

     **"**

— — — — — — — — — — .

What Do You Want to Be When You Grow Up?

What will you be someday? A police officer? A homemaker? An undercover agent? Be sure to ask God to help you choose your career because you'll probably spend most of your time working. Will you be working just for money or will you be serving God by helping people through what you do? *Draw yourself doing the job you think God might want you to do.*

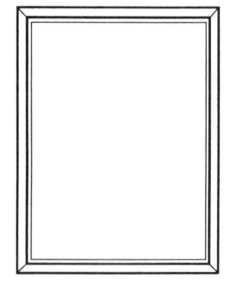

☐ *Draw a star in this box when you've read Matthew 6:24; Luke 16:13-15; Philippians 4:19.*

Store Treasure in Heaven

In Matthew 6:19-21, Jesus talked about storing up treasure in heaven. He wanted His followers to think about and care for things that will last forever. *Use a pencil to write on this treasure chest what you think and care about the most.* Will your "treasures" last forever?

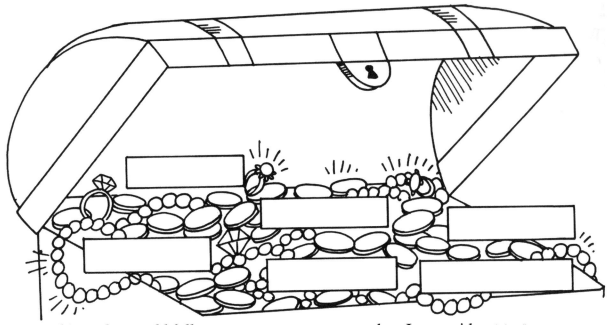

Next, erase things that could fall apart, wear out, or get stolen. Jesus said not to treasure things like that. Instead, He wants us to store up treasure in heaven–what we will care about when we get to heaven. *Write these things in the empty spaces.*

Why did Jesus tell us to store treasure in heaven? *To find Jesus' reason, cross out the letters that spell the picture beside the word.*

YAUOTOMOUBIRLE

MHOENAERYT

WHOIULSLE

BJEEWELRY

WBHOAETRE

TELYEOVUIRSION

TCRLOETAHSEUSRE

ITSOYS

□ *Draw a star in this box when you've read Matthew 6:19-21.*

Serve God with Money

We can trust God to provide everything we need. He also wants us to use everything in our lives to serve Him, including our money. Jesus often warned that riches could get between people and their relationships with God. He said your life isn't made of things you own.

One day Jesus saw a poor widow give two small coins as her offering at the temple. Jesus said she had given more than everyone else because it was all she had to live on. She had learned to trust God to take care of her needs.

Using Money the Right Way

When God blesses you with money, be sure that you don't let it come between you and the Lord. Always use money the way God wants you to use it. *Unscramble these ways money can cause some people problems.*

MEOS EFEL HEYT OD TNO DEEN GDO.

_____

MESO TKHIN EYHT REA TERTEB HANT THERO EPOLEP.

_____

_____

MESO LLIW TON RESHA THWI OHERTS.

_____

SMOE OD TON TEL DGO SEU HERIT NOMEY WOH EH STNAW.

_____

_____

List ways you can serve God with money:

_____

_____

☐ *Draw a star in this box when you've read Matthew 6:25-30; Mark 12:41-44; Luke 12:13-21; 21:1-4; Philippians 4:19.*

Be Sincere

Jesus often scolded some religious leaders for being hypocrites. A hypocrite is someone who pretends to be one thing, but really is another. The religious leaders pretended to love and serve God, when they were really looking out for themselves. These religious leaders said and did all the right things, but for all the wrong reasons. Jesus said the hypocrisy of these leaders was like yeast in bread. Yeast quickly affects the entire loaf of bread. Hypocrisy is the same way. It can spread among people and have a negative influence. Jesus compared hypocrisy to other things, too.

Gnats and Camels

Jesus said that the hypocrites strained their water to keep from swallowing a gnat, but then they swallowed a camel. *Cross out the camels with one hump to find out what He meant.*

Dirty Dishes

Jesus said that the hypocrites cleaned the outside of the cup and dish, but left the inside filthy. He said they should have cleaned the inside of the cup and dish first and then the outside would also be clean. *Cross out the dirty cups to find what Jesus meant.*

Pretty Tombs Full of Dead Bones

Jesus told the hypocrites, "You are like white-washed tombs, which look beautiful on the outside but on the inside are full of dead men's bones." *To find out why they were like tombs, color in the bones that have a dot on them.*

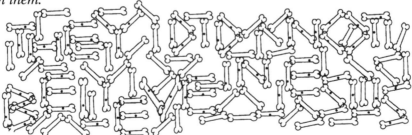

Draw a star in this box when you've read Matthew 16:6-12; 23:24-27; Mark 8:15-21; Luke 12:13; John 1:36.

Right Reasons

In Luke 12:2, 3, Jesus had a warning to people who have secret wrong reasons for what they do and say. *Put the first letter of each word at the end of the word to find out what Jesus said.*

ganythin uyo ehid lwil eb nshow rlate. twha uyo ysa

_____

ni eth kdar lwil eb dhear ni eth tdayligh. twha uyo

_____

rwhispe ni ryou mroo lwil eb dyelle mfro eth froo.

_____

What Are the Right Reasons?

Each picture shows a kid doing something good for the wrong reason. *Cross out what each kid is saying or thinking. Then, below each picture, write a good reason instead.*

I'm going to shovel Miss Edington's sidewalk. She'll think I'm a nice kid and maybe pay me $5.00.

Maybe mom will be so glad I'm cleaning my room that she'll buy me the cassette I want.

I hope all the kids see how much money I'm giving. They'll think I'm really great.

Draw a star in this box when you've read Luke 12:2, 3.

Produce Good Fruit

Good trees produce fruit that is good for people. Trees that are rotten and have gone bad produce fruit that isn't good for people. Jesus said people are like trees. Our attitudes and actions show what kind of people we are. If we're good people, we produce good "fruit."

Jesus said to watch out for leaders who aren't good. He said you can tell whether to follow them by watching what they say and do–"By their fruit you will know them." Jesus wants all of us to produce good fruit.

Fruit of the Spirit

Galatians 5:22, 23 says the Holy Spirit will help God's people to grow these kinds of "fruit" in their lives: love, joy, peace, patience, kindness, goodness, faithfulness, gentleness, and self-control. *Find a trait in each piece of fruit. The letters go in all directions. The first one is done for you.*

☐ *Draw a star in this box when you've read Matthew 16:6-12; 23:24-27; Mark 8:15-21; Luke 12:13; John 1:36.*

Good Ground

Jesus once told a story about a farmer who sowed some seeds. In Bible times, a farmer would usually hold a bag of grain or other seeds and throw them onto the soil. In Jesus' story the seeds landed in these four places.

1. By a path and birds ate them.

2. On rocky places. They sprouted up quickly but shriveled because they didn't have roots.

3. Among thorns, which choked them and kept them from producing fruit.

4. On good ground and produced lots of fruit.

Jesus explained that this is like what happens when people hear the Word of God. If a person believes in Jesus and welcomes Him into his or her life, that person's faith will grow and take root—that person will serve God. But sometimes other things keep a person's faith from taking root. *Match the people to the pictures and put the correct number in each box. If you need help, look in Matthew 13:18-23.*

I have too much to worry about. I don't have time to pray or serve God.

My faith in Jesus is growing and I love to serve Him.

Somebody told me about Jesus once. I didn't understand.

I was excited about becoming a Christian, but when people teased me about it, I gave up.

☐ A

☐ B

☐ C

☐ D

Which kind of ground are you? Write the number here: _____.

☐ *Draw a star in this box when you've read Matthew 13:3-8, 18-23; Mark 4:3-8, 14-20: and Luke 8:5-8, 11-15.*

Be Careful Who You Follow

Some people who are leaders don't really know Jesus. They try to lead other people when they don't know where they're going themselves. *Use the Braille code to find out what Jesus says about this in Matthew 7:15 and 15:14.*

a	BRAILLE CODE			
b	c	d	e	f
g	h	i	j	k
l	m	n	o	p
q	r	s	t	u
v	w	x	y	z

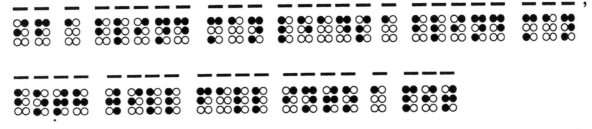

Make a Wolf-in-Sheep Puppet

Jesus said to watch out for some people who pretend to be sheep following Jesus, the Good Shepherd, but who are really like wolves on the inside, waiting to harm the sheep.

What You Need

- 2 disposable cups
- scissors
- cotton balls
- glue
- permanent markers
- scraps of brown felt or paper
- tape

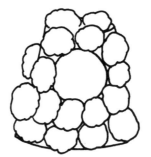

What You Do

1. Cut a large hole as shown in the cup used for the sheep. Glue cotton balls all over the cup.

2. Insert the wolf cup inside the sheep cup. Draw a wolf face on the cup as shown. Pull out the wolf cup, cut small triangles for ears, and tape the ears to the wolf as shown.

☐ *Draw a star in this box when you've read Matthew 7:15; 15:14.*

Be Sure It's in the Bible

Jesus said that some people make up rules and treat these rules as if they're God's commands. These rules can get in the way of a person doing what is right. Some people think that keeping extra rules about how you live or what you eat or drink makes you a good person. Some of these rules are good advice, but they are not commandments from God. Jesus said that obeying these rules isn't what makes a person good, but what comes out of a person's heart does.

Always be sure the things you believe are really found in the Bible. When you want to learn about a certain topic, such as "faith" or "love" in the Bible, you can look it up in a concordance. A *concordance* tells you which Bible verses use that specific word.

Is It in the Bible?

A concordance is a great tool to help you find things in the Bible. Words are listed in alphabetical order. When you find the word you are looking for, you will see a list of Bible passages that have used the word in them. *Use a concordance to find out which of these animals are mentioned in the Bible. If you have never used a concordance before, ask a grown-up to help you.*

Yes   No   Yes   No   Yes   No

Yes   No   Yes   No   Yes   No

Draw a star in this box when you've read Matthew 15:9; Mark 7:7, 13, 18-23.

Remember What's Important

Mary and Martha

Jesus went to visit two sisters named Mary and Martha. Mary sat at Jesus' feet and listened to Him. But Martha was very busy preparing for their guest. Martha asked Jesus, "Lord, don't You care that my sister isn't helping me serve? Tell her to help me." Jesus said, "Martha, you are too careful and worried about many things. Only one thing is needed. Mary has chosen that. It won't be taken away from her."

Decode What Martha Learned

= A   = F   = N   = T

= B   = H   = 0   = U

= D   = L   = R   = Y

= E   = M   = S

Message:

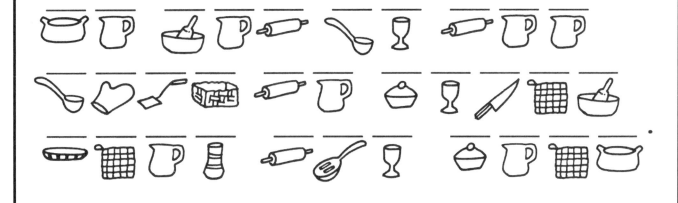

Draw a star in this box when you've read Luke 10:38-42.

Daily Planner

Spending time with God is one of the most important things you can do. *Write in when you will pray and study the Bible each day. Then fill in your other activities.*

	SUN	MON	TUE	WED	THU	FRI	SAT
7:00							
7:30							
8:00							
8:30							
9:00							
9:30							
10:00							
10:30							
11:00							
11:30							
NOON							
12:30							
1:00							
1:30							
2:00							
2:30							
3:00							
3:30							
4:00							
4:30							
5:00							
5:30							
6:00							
6:30							
7:00							
7:30							
8:00							
8:30							
9:00							

Keep Your Good Deeds Secret

Jesus said not to do good deeds in front of people to try to make them think you are good. If you do, you won't be rewarded by your Father in heaven. Don't tell people when you give to the needy. People who do that have already received their reward. Jesus said not to even let your left hand know what your right hand is doing. Do good things secretly and God will reward you openly.

Make Handprint Pictures

To remind you not to let your left hand know what your right hand is doing, trace your hands on other sheets of paper and then add details to make these pictures.

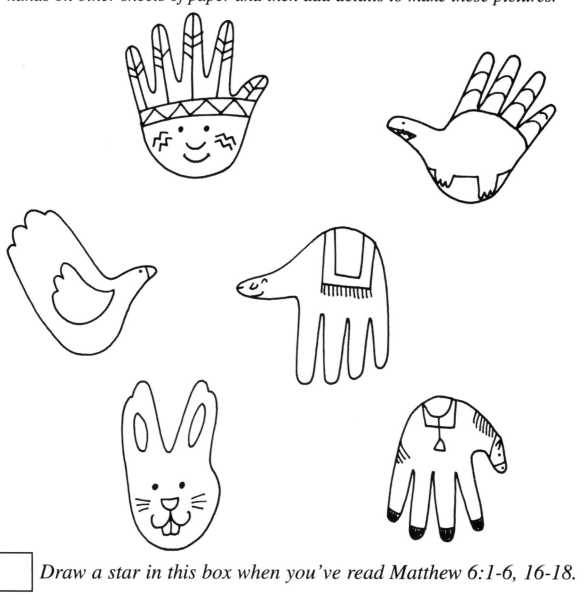

Draw a star in this box when you've read Matthew 6:1-6, 16-18.

Get Rid of What Causes Sin

Jesus wants us to do what's right. He said we should get rid of what causes us to do wrong things. In fact, Jesus said that we would be better off without our hands, feet, or eyes than for us to let them cause us to sin. Now, He didn't mean we should actually get rid of our hands, feet, and eyes. He was pointing out that sometimes there are things that we <u>think</u> are necessary, but if they cause us to sin, they aren't really necessary and we should get rid of them.

Put the initial from each ring in the blanks with the same number as the hand wearing the ring. You will discover some things that may cause you to do wrong things.

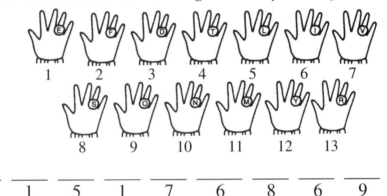

__	__	__	__	__	__	__	__	__	__
4	1	5	1	7	6	8	6	9	10

How might this cause you to sin?

__	__	__	__	__	__	__
2	13	6	1	10	3	8

How might this cause you to sin?

__	__	__	__	__
11	9	10	1	12

How might this cause you to sin?

Can you think of other things that may seem necessary, but actually could cause you to sin?

_____

☐ *Draw a star in this box when you've read Matthew 18:7-9 and Mark 9:43-47.*

Count the Cost

A Man Building a Tower

In Luke 14:28-33, Jesus asked some questions. "Doesn't a man building a tower figure out how much it will cost before he begins? Otherwise people will make fun of him when they see he wasn't able to finish what he started."

A King Going to Battle

Jesus also asked, "Doesn't a king fighting a war against another king figure out whether he has enough men to win? If he doesn't have enough, he will ask the other king what he wants so they can prevent a war."

Someone Wanting to Follow Jesus

Jesus said, "In the same way, any of you who does not give up everything he has cannot be my disciple." To become Jesus' followers, we must trust our very lives to Him. Will we give Him all of our time? Will we use all of our money the way He wants? Will we be willing to do whatever He asks?

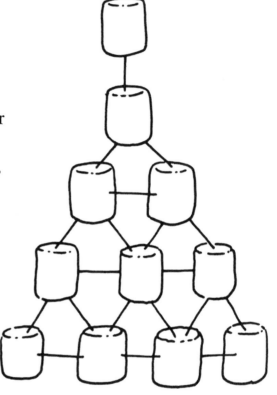

Build this tower with marshmallows & toothpicks. Before you begin, count how many marshmallows and toothpicks you will need. Check the number in the answers on page 129. Have you thought about what it will take to follow Jesus? Will you trust Him with everything in your life?

Draw a star in this box when you've read Luke 14:28-33.

Don't Look Back

One day when Jesus asked some people to follow Him, all had reasons why they couldn't go right then. Jesus said that no one who puts his hand to the plow and looks back is ready to serve Him. Plowing breaks up hard soil to make it easier for a seed to get in and grow. Jesus wants us to love others like He does; this softens their hard hearts so they are ready to receive Him as Lord and Savior.

Plow on Paper

A plow makes straight rows in a field like lines on notebook paper. *Pretend your pen is a plow and trace the lines on this page. Halfway across each line, look over your shoulder and keep drawing. What happens? If you keep going while looking back, you do a poor job. If you stop while looking back, the work doesn't get done.*

Decode this message by changing every A to E, every E to A, every I to O, and every O to I.

Dacoda ti sarva Jasus end than din't sliw diwn ir stip.

Din't avar thonk ebiut giong beck ti tha lofa yiu hed

bafira yiu eskad Jasus ti ba yiur Lird.

☐ *Draw a star in this box when you've read Luke 9:57-62.*

Give God What Is His

Some people asked Jesus if they should pay money to the Roman leader, Caesar. Jesus told them to show Him a coin used to pay the tax to Rome. When they brought Jesus a coin called a denarius, He asked whose image and name was on the coin. They said, "Caesar's." Jesus said, "Give to Caesar what is Caesar's and to God what is God's."

1. The denarius coin was made with Caesar's image on it. Who was made in God's image? (Gen. 1:27)

_____

2. The coin had Caesar's name on it. If you are a Christian, what name is on you?

_____

Make a Picture Frame to Say You Belong to God

What You Need

- two 3" x 5" cards and a stand (use the pattern)
- photo of you
- ruler
- pencil
- scissors
- tape
- 3" x 5" piece of clear plastic (such as from a report cover)
- glue

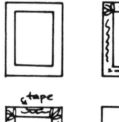

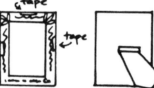

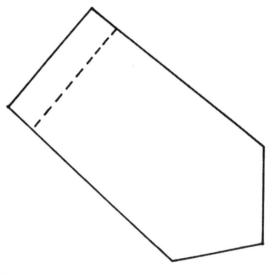

What You Do

1. *Draw a rectangle 3/4 inch inside the edges of the 3" x 5" card that will be the front of the frame. Cut it out.*
2. *Write "I belong to God" across the bottom of the frame front.*
3. *Color a design around the front of the frame.*
4. *Lay the frame on top of the plastic piece and then lay these on top of the uncut card. Tape these together on the top and sides, leaving the bottom untaped.*
5. *Slide in photo between the plastic and the back of the frame. If it won't fit, trim a little off the edges.*
6. *Bend the stand. Glue the top part of the stand to the back of the frame as shown. Let it dry.*

☐ *Draw a star in this box when you've read Matthew 22:15-22; Mark 12:13-17; Luke 20:19-26.*

I DID IT!

COMPLETED	DATE	COMPLETED	DATE
☐ The Work God Wants	_____	☐ Make Clothespin Puppets	_____
☐ Keep the Faith	_____	☐ The Rich Young Man	_____
☐ Love with All Your Heart	_____	☐ Choose Your Master	_____
☐ Be Born Again	_____	☐ Store Treasure in Heaven	_____
☐ My Birth Announcements	_____	☐ Serve God with Money	_____
☐ Join the Family	_____	☐ Be Sincere	_____
☐ Get on the Narrow Road	_____	☐ Right Reasons	_____
☐ The Old and the New	_____	☐ Produce Good Fruit	_____
☐ Build Your House on the Rock	_____	☐ Good Ground	_____
☐ Love Each Other	_____	☐ Be Careful Who You Follow	_____
☐ Tell the Good News	_____	☐ Be Sure It's in the Bible	_____
☐ Make a T-Shirt to Help with the Harvest	_____	☐ Remember What's Important	_____
☐ Jesus' Overpaid Workers	_____	☐ Daily Planner	_____
☐ Let Your Light Shine	_____	☐ Keep Your Good Deeds Secret	_____
☐ A Bright Reminder	_____	☐ Get Rid of What Causes Sin	_____
☐ Be Salty	_____	☐ Count the Cost	_____
☐ The Prodigal Son	_____	☐ Don't Look Back	_____
☐ Help the Poor	_____	☐ Give God What Is His	_____

Learning to Love Like Jesus

A New Commandment

In John 13:34, 35, Jesus gave His disciples a new commandment to follow. They were to love each other as He loved them.

Make Heart-Stamped Bible Verse Cards about Love

What You Need

- potato
- pencil
- plastic knife
- paintbrush
- red paint
- markers
- at least three index or blank recipe cards

What You Do

1. *Cut the potato in half and draw a heart on the potato. Using the knife, carefully carve away the part of the potato around the heart.*
2. *Brush red paint on the heart and then press it on each card. Decorate the card.*
3. *Look up these Bible passages about love: Matthew 5:43-46; 22:37-39; and John 13:34-36. Write them on the cards.*

Memorize these verses. Ask God to help you follow His commandment to love one another.

Make a Bible Verse Card Stand

What You Need

- clean, empty plastic detergent bottle
- ruler
- permanent marker
- scissors

Make a stand for your Bible Verse Cards. Put your verse cards about love on the stand and place it on your desk or dresser. As you get ready for school, pull a card out of the stand and practice memorizing that verse.

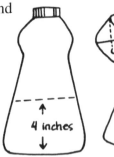

What You Do

1. *Soak the bottle in warm water until the label peels off easily.*
2. *Poke a hole in the bottle about 3 inches from the top. Stick the scissors through the hole and cut off the top of the bottle.*
3. *Next, measure 4 inches from the bottom of the bottle and draw a line around the bottle. Cut the bottle along that line.*
4. *Draw slanted lines on the sides of the stand as shown. Draw a notch where the cards will sit, and then draw a straight line across the front. Cut along the lines.*
5. *Draw hearts on the front of the stand. Store your verse cards in the stand.*

☐ *Draw a star in this box when you've read Matthew 5:43-46; 22:37-39; and John 13:34, 35.*

Make a Tin Punch Pie Plate

Here's another reminder to love one another as Jesus did. Follow these directions to make a tin punch pie plate of Jesus' new commandment.

What You Need

- 9-inch disposable aluminum pie plate
- newspaper
- pattern from this page (you can trace it or make a photocopy)
- masking tape
- a pushpin
- liquid shoe polish, any color
- silver duct tape
- paper clip

What You Do

1. *Place the pie plate on a stack of newspapers. Next, tape the pattern from this page into the pie plate.*
2. *Carefully poke the pushpin through each dot of the pattern. Then remove the pattern and tape.*
3. *Dab shoe polish on the pie plate to make it look antique.*
4. *Use duct tape to attach a paper clip to the back for hanging.*

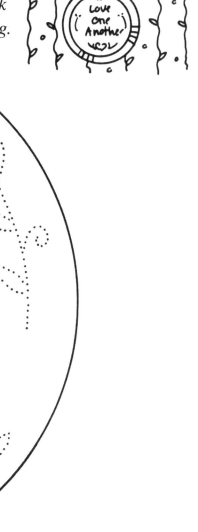

Love One Another

The Golden Rule

In Luke 6:31, Jesus said, "Do to others as you would have them do to you." In other words, treat people the way you would want them to treat you. Some people call this the "golden rule." Make a golden ruler and practice treating others the way you would like to be treated.

Make a Golden Ruler

What You Need

- 12-inch ruler
- cardboard box
- gold spray paint, silver spray paint (or another color besides gold)
- alphabet macaroni
- glue
- scissors
- spray lacquer

What You Do

1. *Lay the ruler inside the cardboard box. Spray paint the front of the ruler gold and let it dry. When the front is dry, turn the ruler over and spray paint the other side gold.*
2. *While the ruler is drying, use the macaroni alphabet letters to spell out "Do to others as you would have them do to you." Spray paint the letters silver or another color. Let them dry.*
3. *When both the ruler and letters are completely dry, place the letters on the ruler to get the correct spacing between words. Then glue each letter to the front of the ruler. Let the glue dry.*
4. *Copy the message below, cut it out, and glue it to the back of the ruler.*
5. *Spray both sides of the ruler with lacquer. Let dry.*

DO TO OTHERS AS YOU WOULD HAVE THEM DO TO YOU.

How to Use Your Golden Ruler

As a family or with a group of friends, agree that for the next couple of days, all of you will treat others as you would like to be treated. To do this, think of how you would like to be treated or think of something that would make you happy, then secretly do it for someone else, and leave the ruler where that person can find it. Within 24 hours that person should do something for someone else. Even when you don't have the golden ruler, keep treating others the way you want to be treated.

Draw a star in this box when you've read the story in Luke 6:31.

Practice the Golden Rule

The Golden Rule is easy to remember but a lot harder to practice. Read each of these situations and think about ways to practice treating others as you would want to be treated.

How do you feel when you need to make a phone call and someone is on the phone?

1. How can you practice the golden rule when you're talking on the phone and someone else wants to use it?

If you had a hard day and then got mad at your brother or sister, what would you want him or her to do? Yell at you? Tattle on you? Forgive you?

2. How can you practice the golden rule when someone gets angry at you?

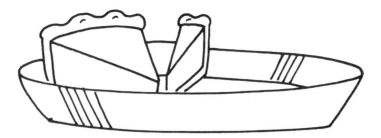

3. Suppose you're handing out the pieces of pie. According to the golden rule, which should you offer your sister?

There are two pieces of pie left. Your sister is ready to hand out the last two pieces of pie—one's big and the other's small. Which piece would you like her to offer you?

How do you feel when your brother or sister borrows your things without asking?

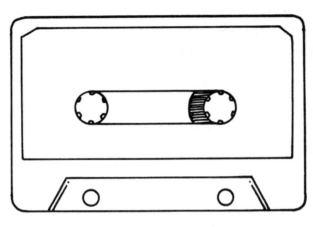

4. If you were practicing the golden rule, what would you do if you wanted to listen to your brother's tapes?

You're watching TV and your brother comes into the room. He's not interested in the show you're watching. What would you want him to do?

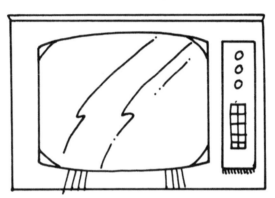

5. How would you practice the golden rule if your brother was watching a TV show you didn't like?

Give Warm Fuzzies

Some people describe a "warm fuzzy" as a feeling of being loved. *Make this "warm fuzzy" critter to give to someone. All you have to do is glue plastic eyes or felt eyes to a fuzzy pom-pom. Look for these materials in a craft store. Send a note along with your "warm fuzzy" that says how much you care for this person and what you like best about him or her.*

WARM FUZZY

I love you, Mom. I think you're the best Mom in the whole world.

The Good Samaritan

In Luke 10:30-37, Jesus told a story in answer to a man's question. The man knew that God's law said to love God wholeheartedly and to love your neighbor as yourself. The man asked Jesus who his neighbor was, and Jesus told the story of the Good Samaritan. *Take the extra letter out of each word to read the story Jesus told.*

At mane woent froom Jerustalem tot Jjericho. Thievers atttacked hime, trore boff hist cloothes, sand lefst shim hoalf dread.

Ar pariest hoappened toe comet theat sway mand wohen dhe staw tehe shurt manx, her pastsed bye thim lon ther mother stide wof them troad.

At Lrevite alsos crame bay, slooked bat ther shurt mant, dand spassed bey pon thex bother stide.

Bute la Sqamaritan (ar manc froom aa sneighboring countlry, whosee speople wered thated byr thes Jewsz) crame swhere thev shurt mani wase, land wahen hev sawd thim, hbe lhad crompassion fort fhim.

Thes Sbamaritan wentl tov himo, clfeaned ande bandoaged mhis wrounds, agnd sput bhim pon lhis sown ranimal. Hew brorught thes sinjured mane tov ran minn, band stook caret lof fhim.

Theb snext dray wahen sthe Slamaritan leeft, hhe grave them binnkeeper wsome mnoney rand staid, "Trake scare cof hirm; kand whatlever moret youv spends, I'lll pray youv whern Id treturn."

Theno Jresus masked at mane, "Whirch lof thez threet wast ar nelighbor tot thew victims?" Thec mant fanswered, "Thew bone whot slhowed mercy tox hime." Jesust staid, "Goe hand dot them samet."

Draw a star in this box when you've read the story in Luke 10:30-37.

Tell the Good Samaritan Story with Puppets

Jesus told the story of the Good Samaritan to help people understand that loving your "neighbor" means caring for people no matter who they are. *Make some egg puppets and use the puppets to perform this story.*

What You Need

- seven hard-boiled eggs
- waterproof markers

What You Do

1. Rinse and dry the cool boiled eggs.

2. Use the markers to draw faces on the eggs. See the illustrations for the kinds of faces to draw for the characters in the story.

3. Move the eggs around as you tell the story of the Good Samaritan.

Two Robbers

The Victim

The Levite

The Priest

The Samaritan

The Innkeeper

Love Your Neighbor as Yourself

In Matthew 22:37-39, Jesus said the first and greatest commandment was to love the Lord God with all your heart, soul, and mind. And He said the second is to love your neighbor as you love yourself. Your neighbors aren't just the people who live on your street. A neighbor can be anyone you may meet. Try to make a new friend each day. Make this Buddy-a-Day calendar and have fun making new friends.

Buddy-a-Day Calendar

Number this calendar to match the month that's coming up next. Begin this activity on the first day of the month. Each day try to get to know someone you haven't talked with very much in the past. Write that person's name on the square for that date, or have the person autograph that square. By the end of the month, you'll be pleased to see how many new "neighbors" you've met.

SUNDAY	MONDAY	TUESDAY	WEDNESDAY	THURSDAY	FRIDAY	SATURDAY

Draw a star in this box when you've read Matthew 22:37-39.

Include Others

Suppose your mom said you could invite some people over to spend the night. Who would you invite? Your friends, of course—who else is there to invite? In Luke 14:12-14, Jesus said that there are other people to include, people who might not be at all like you. People who belong to the out group and can't ever return the invitation. But that's what loving Jesus is all about—including everyone, no matter what. Here is a fun idea for an "in" party—that's a party in which you include other people you usually don't hang around with.

Plan a Cookie Pizza Party

First get you parents' permission to have a party. Then plan a cookie pizza party for after school. Invite your friends as well as people who don't usually get invited to parties. Introduce them to your friends.

When each guest arrives, give him or her a fruit to prepare for the pizza. God will bless you for having the courage to reach out to lonely people.

What You Need

- sugar cookie dough
  (homemade or purchased)
- cream cheese frosting (homemade or purchased)
- different fruit of your choice (at least one kind for each guest)
- knives for slicing fruit
- grown-up help

What You Do

1. *Preheat the oven to the temperature in the recipe on the package. Spread the cookie dough onto a lightly buttered pizza pan. Bake until golden (see the recipe or package for the amount of time. Check often).*
2. *When the dough is done baking, let it cool. Then spread a thin layer of cream cheese frosting on the cookie crust.*
3. *Let everyone arrange their slices of fruit on it however they wish.*
4. *Cut the "pizza" into thin slices and enjoy eating.*

☐ *Draw a star in this box when you've read Luke 14:12-14.*

The Least of These

In Matthew 25:31-46, Jesus talks about a scene that will take place in the future, after He comes back for His followers. But there's something we can learn from this passage and practice right now, before Jesus comes back. It has to do with our attitude and what we do for people who have needs. *Correct the spacing to read this story. The first line is done for you.*

The|Son|of|God|will|sit|on|a|throne|and|say|to|some|of|the|people|"Come,|youwhoareblessedbyMyFather,inheritakingdomthatwaspreparedforyou whentheworldwascreated.IwashungryandyougaveMesomethingtoeat.Iwasth irstyandyougaveMesomethingtodrink.IwasastrangerandyouinvitedMein. IwasnakedandyouclothedMe.IwassickandyoulookedafterMe.Iwasinprisona ndyoucametoMe."

Thenthosewhoarerighteouswillsay,"WhendidwedothosethingsforYou?"The Kingwillanswer,"WhenyoudiditfortheleastofMybrothers,youdiditforMe."

JesussaidtheotherswillbepunishedfornothelpingHimwhenHewasinneed. They'llsay,"WhendidweseeYouinneedandwedidn'thelpYou?"He'llsay, "Whenyoudidn'thelptheleastofMybrothers,youdidn'thelpMe."Jesussaidtho sewhodidn'thelpHimwillgotoeverlastingpunishment,butthosewhowere righteouswillgotolivewithGodforever.

☐ *Draw a star in this box when you've read Matthew 25:31-46.*

Help Others and Help Jesus

Jesus said that if you're helping people in need, you're helping Him. There is plenty for you to do even though you're young and even if you don't have a lot of money. Here are some ideas.

• Pray and ask God to show you people who need your help.

• Ask your parents if your family can contribute food to a food pantry or to a church group that feeds the poor. Maybe your family could take a meal to a family in which the parents are out of work. Ask if you can give away clothes you no longer wear or buy some new ones for people who need them.

• Ask your Sunday school teacher or another church leader if your class can plan a project to help people who are poor, sick, or lonely.

• You might plan a short visit to a classmate who has been sick. Or you could send a card to someone in the hospital.

Make a Bed Table for Someone Sick

What You Need

• a strong box that is wider than a person's lap
• scissors or knife
• Con-Tact paper
• goodies for the box
• grown-up help if needed

What You Do

1. *Using either the scissors or the knife, cut away parts of the sides as shown in the illustration. You want the box to be able to fit over a person's lap. If it is too hard for you to cut the box yourself, ask a grown-up for help.*

2. *Cover the box with Con-Tact paper.*

3. *To make the table an extra special surprise, turn it upside down and line it with tissue paper. Then fill it with different get-well goodies. For example, lemons for making hot lemonade, comic books or magazines, puzzle or activity books, homemade stationery, and a homemade get-well card.*

Jesus Washed His Disciples' Feet

In John 13:1-17, Jesus set an example of serving others. In Bible times, because the roads were dusty and dirty, servants washed the feet of guests when they entered the host's home. When the disciples came to an upper room for the Passover supper, there was no servant to wash their feet. And certainly none of them would stoop to do a servant's work and wash feet. That's when Jesus began His lesson about serving. *Read each word backward. Then color the picture.*

sA eht revossaP reppus saw gnieb devres, suseJ koot ffo siH retuo sehtolc, depparw a lewot dnuora siH tsiaw, dna deruop retaw ni a egral lwob. nehT eH detrats gnihsaw eht 'selpicsid teef dna gniyrd meht no eht lewot taht saw depparw dnuora miH.

nehW ti saw nomiS s'reteP nrut, eh t'ndid tnaw suseJ ot hsaw sih teef. suseJ dias, "sselnU I hsaw uoy, uoy evah on trap htiw eM." reteP dias, "toN tsuj ym teef tub ym sdnah dna ym daeh sa llew." suseJ dias enoemos ohw sah dah a htab ylno sdeen sih teef dehsaw ot eb yletelpmoc naelc. eH dias, "uoY era naelc, hguoht ton yreve eno fo uoy." eH dias taht esuaceb eH wenk saduJ toiracsI saw gniog ot nrut tsniaga miH dna llet dab elpoep erehw ot dnif miH.

drawretfA, suseJ desserd dna tas nwod niaga. eH deksa, "oD uoy dnatsrednu tahw I evah enod rof uoy? uoY llac eM rehcaeT dna droL, dna ylthgir os rof taht si tahw I ma. woN taht I, ruoy droL dna rehcaeT, evah dehsaw ruoy teef, uoy osla dluohs hsaw eno s'rehtona teef. I evah tes uoy na elpmaxe taht uoy dluohs od sa I evah enod rof uoy. I llet uoy eht hturt, on tnavres si retaerg naht sih retsam, ron si a regnessem retaerg naht eht eno ohw tnes mih. woN taht uoy wonk eseht sgniht, uoy lliw eb desselb fi uoy od meht."

Show that you're willing to serve, and offer to give your mom or dad a foot massage. Rub lotion on the feet. Your parents will enjoy the extra treat, especially after a hard day.

☐ *Draw a star in this box when you've read John 13:1-17.*

Jump at the Chance to Serve God

Jesus had a lot to say about serving others. In Matthew 20:25-28; Mark 9:33-35; and Mark 10:43-45 Jesus gave a different definition of being great or being first. Jesus said that true greatness comes through serving others. This project will remind you to "hop" right to it when it comes to serving God.

What You Need

• 4 pipe cleaners (chenille wires)

• index cards, cut in half

What You Do

1. Bend the pipe cleaners into a bunny shape as shown in the illustration. Also bend the bunny's paws so they hold the cards.

2. Take time to pray and ask the Lord to show you different ways you can serve others. As you think of some ideas, write them on the cards. When you do serve the Lord in one of the ways, take that card out of the bunny's paws. To keep the bunny's paws full, keep asking God to help you find ways to serve your family, friends, neighbors, and other people you know.

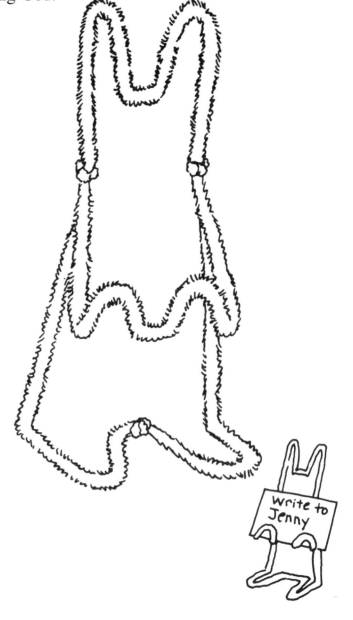

write to Jenny

[ ] *Draw a star in this box when you've read Matthew 20:25-28; Mark 9:33-35; 10:43-45.*

The Forgiven Servant Who Didn't Forgive

One time Peter came to Jesus and asked Him how many times he should forgive someone. Jesus then told this story about true forgiveness. *To read this story from Matthew 18:22-35, change the letters so E is A and A is E. Change them so O is U and U is O.*

Tha kingdum uf haevan is lika e king whu hed e sarvent thet uwad him milliums of dullers. Tha sarvent cuoldn't pey su tha king wes guing tu heva tha men end his femily suld intu slevary. Ell uf tha men's pussassiuns wara tu ba suld, elsu. Bot tha sarvent baggad tha king tu ba petiant with him end seid ha wuold pey it ell. Tha king falt surry fur tha sarvent, furgeva him, end seid ha didn't heva tu pey.

When tha sarvent laft tha king, tha sarvent grebbad e men by tha thruet whu uwad him moch lass then ha hed uwad tha king. Tha sarvent damendad thet tha men pey right than. Tha men baggad tha sarvent just es tha sarvent hed baggad tha king. Bot tha sarvent hed tha men pot in jeil.

Whan tha king haerd ebuot it, ha wes vary engry baceosa ha hed shuwn marcy tu tha sarvent bot tha sarvent hedn't shuwn marcy tu uthars. Tha king sant tha men tu ba turtorad ontil ha hed peid avarything ha hed uwad. Jasos seid this is whet uor haevanly Fethar will du tu os if wa dun't furgiva uor bruthars frum uor haerts.

Unscramble why we should forgive others:

OGD ASH ROFVIGNE SU.

Draw a star in this box when you've read Matthew 18:22-35.

Erase Unforgiveness from Your Heart

When you are alone, use a pencil to write inside this heart the names of people you need to forgive. Pray and ask God to get rid of your hurt and anger. When your bad feelings toward each person are gone, erase that person's name off the list until all of the unforgiveness is gone from your heart.

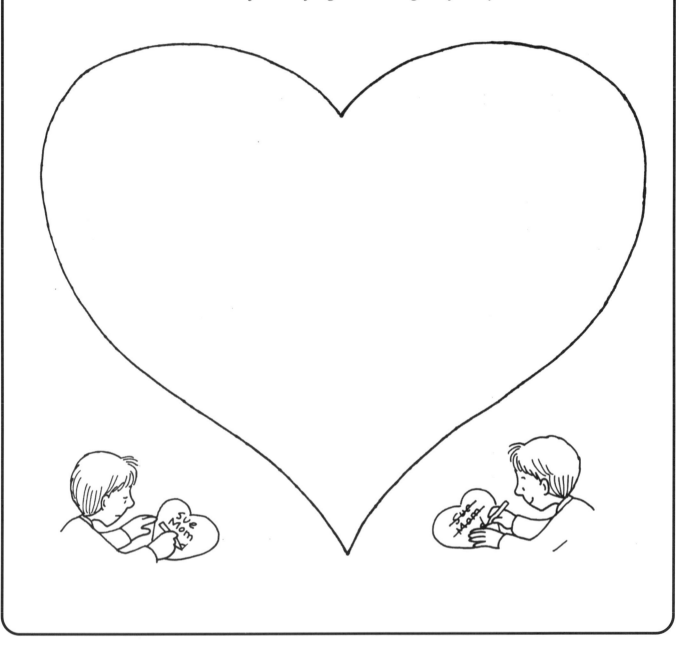

Unlimited Forgiveness

Simon Peter asked Jesus how many times he should forgive his brother who sinned against him. Peter suggested seven times, but Jesus answered seventy times seven. Now, Jesus didn't mean 490 times and that's it—no more forgiveness. He wanted Peter to understand that even if someone keeps doing things that hurt you, God wants you to keep forgiving.

Find the Path to Forgiveness

Lightly draw a line along the path that runs from the angry kids to where they have made up with each other. Vowels along the correct path will help complete the sentences at the bottom of the page. Write the first vowel in the blank of the first sentence and continue until all the sentences are completed.

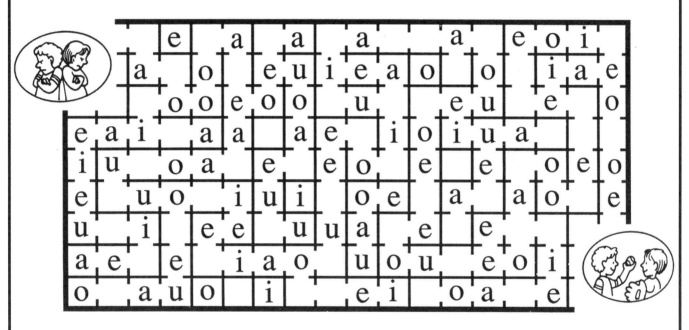

1. Pr__y f__r G__d t__ t__k__ __w__y y__ __ __ r __nf__rg__v__n__ss.

2. Th__nk __b__ __t why th__ p__rs__n d__d wh__t sh__ d__d.

3. T__lk __b__ __t th__ pr__bl__m wh__n y__ __'r__ b__th c__lm.

4. Try t__ l__v__ th__ p__rs__n l__k__ G__d d__ __s.

☐ *Draw a star in this box when you've read Matthew 18:21, 22.*

Make Up Quickly

In Matthew 5:23-26, Jesus said if someone was bringing a gift to God at the altar and remembered that someone was mad at him or her, that person should go and make things right before worshiping God. Jesus said it is important to make things right with someone quickly. Later Paul wrote in Ephesians 4:26 that you shouldn't let the sun go down while you're still angry. Make this setting sun and hang it in your room to remind you to make up quickly with people.

Make a Setting Sun

What You Need

- twine
- scissors
- plastic wrap
- glue
- paper cup
- orange, gold, or red glitter
- paper plate

What You Do

1. *Unwind some twine and measure it out according to this picture. You want enough twine to outline the sun and its rays. When you have the correct length, cut the twine.*
2. *Lay plastic wrap over this page.*
3. *Pour two or three tablespoons of glue into the cup. Dip the piece of twine in the glue.*
4. *Pour some glitter on the paper plate, and lay the twine in it. Turn the string over so both sides are coated.*
5. *Next, carefully place the glitter-covered twine on the plastic, in the shape of the sun.*
6. *When the twine design is completely dry, carefully lift the plastic and hold it over a trash can. Gently remove the plastic, letting extra glitter fall into the trash can.*
7. *Use thread and a thumbtack or pushpin to hang your twine design from the ceiling.*

Draw a star in this box when you've read Matthew 5:23-26 and Ephesians 4:26.

Love Everyone...

In Matthew 5:44-47 and Luke 6:32-35, Jesus said to love your enemies, to do good to those who hate you, and to pray for those who are mean to you on purpose. God makes the sun rise on both the evil people and the good. He sends rain on both the just and the unjust. He said you shouldn't just love those who love you; you should love everyone.

Love All of Your Classmates at School

•On the squares below, write the names of all of your classmates under the faces. Next, add hair, glasses, and other details to make the faces look like your classmates.

•Now think about each person and ask yourself, "Does this person know that I like him or her?" If you can honestly answer yes, draw a heart around that person's head.

•Ask the Lord to help you love everyone in your class—even people who are hard to love. Look for things to admire about each person. Be nice to each person.

•As you genuinely learn to like each person and you show it enough that the person knows you like him or her by your actions, draw a heart around each of the other faces.

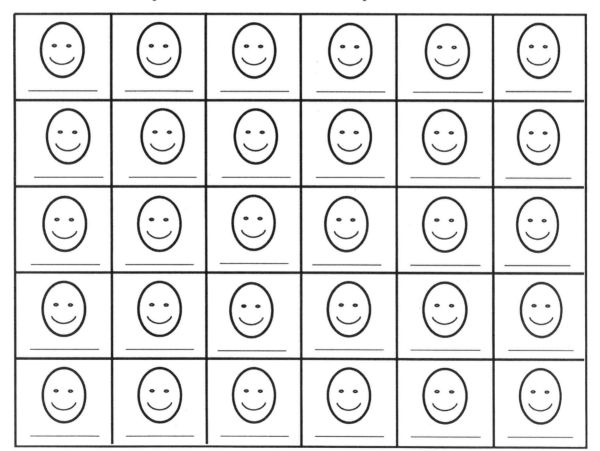

Draw a star in this box when you've read Matthew 5:44-47 and Luke 6:32-35.

The Good News

It's good news to know that God forgives our sins and we can live with Him because Jesus died for our sins and came back to life. The greatest way to show love for people is to tell them about Jesus.

Before you can tell this good news, there's one important question you have to answer: Have you trusted Jesus to forgive you and allow you to live forever with God? You can trust Jesus by praying a prayer like this:

Dear God,

I've done wrong things, and I'm sorry. Please forgive me. I believe Jesus died for my sins and that He came back to life.

I trust You to forgive my sins. I want to follow You all of my life. Thank You for forgiving me and letting me live with You forever because of Jesus. I love You.

In Jesus' name. Amen.

Now that you believe in Jesus, you have some good news to tell everyone. In Mark 16:15, Jesus told His followers to do the same. Here is one way you can tell a friend about Jesus.

Personalize a Bible for a Friend

What You Need

- paperback Bible
- piece of stationery
- picture of yourself
- pen or pencil
- wrapping paper
- gluestick

What You Do

1. *Save your money and buy an inexpensive Bible for your friend.*
2. *When you have a Bible, cut a piece of stationery to fit inside the front cover.*
3. *Glue your picture to the piece of stationery and write a letter telling your friend how much you like reading the Bible and learning about Jesus. Also tell your friend that you know Jesus loves him or her and that God will forgive your friend's sins so he or she can go to heaven if your friend trusts Jesus as the only way. Offer to pray with your friend about it.*
4. *Gift wrap the Bible and give it to your friend.*

Draw a star in this box when you've read Mark 16:15.

Jesus Ate with Sinners

In Jesus' day, the Pharisees looked down on people they considered "sinners." The Pharisees thought they were better than everyone else because they strictly followed God's laws—and even added some of their own to follow. They would never dream of eating with these so-called sinners. Jesus, however, had a different opinion. In Matthew 9:10-13, Jesus and the disciples were having dinner with these "sinners," when the Pharisees asked why Jesus ate with these kind of people. Jesus said that He didn't come for people who thought they were good enough, but He came to encourage sinners to come to Him.

Jesus doesn't want us to look down our noses at people who don't follow Him or people who are really different from us. He wants us to love them and show them His love, too.

What You Need

- 6 slices of white bread
- white school glue
- 1/2 teaspoon dishwashing liquid
- water
- toothpick
- paintbrush and paint
- newspaper
- lacquer
- two 24-inch pieces of twine or ribbon
- scissors
- mirror

Make a Funny Nose

A reminder that it's silly to to be snooty to people.

What You Do

1. *Tear the crusts off the bread and feed them to the birds.*
2. *Crumble the rest of the bread into tiny pieces in a bowl. Add 6 teaspoons of glue and 1/2 teaspoon dishwashing liquid.*
3. *Stir with a spoon until mixed. Then mix the dough with your hands until it isn't sticky. If it's too dry, add a few more drops of glue. If it's too sticky, add part of another slice of bread.*
4. *Shape the dough to fit loosely on your nose (it will shrink a little as it dries). Shape it to make your nose look extra long. Turn it up at the end. Use the toothpick to poke a small hole on each side of the nose for the strings.*
5. *When your funny nose is finished, paint it with a mixture of 4 tablespoons of glue and 4 tablespoons of water. This will help prevent cracking.*
6. *When the nose is completely dry, paint it wild colors. Let it dry and spray it with lacquer.*
7. *Tie a piece of twine or ribbon through each hole. Place the nose on your face and tie the twine or ribbons behind your head. You're ready to show how silly it is to be snooty.*

Draw a star in this box when you've read Matthew 9:10-13.

The Speck and the Plank

Have you ever noticed that it's very easy to see other people's faults, but it's hard to see our faults and sins even when our faults and sins are much bigger than theirs? In Matthew 7:3-5 and Luke 6:41, 42, Jesus talked about the same thing, comparing a speck of sawdust to a plank. Jesus asked His listeners why they look at a speck of sawdust in another person's eye, but they don't notice the plank in their own eyes. He asked how a person could say, "Brother, let me pull out the speck that's in your eye" when that person can't even see the board that's in his own eye. Jesus called this kind of person a "hypocrite" (someone who pretends to be one thing, but actually is something else). Jesus' message to this kind of person: "First take the plank out of your eye, and then you will see clearly to remove the speck from your brother's eye."

Draw a Cartoon

Draw yourself with a board in your eye trying to help someone with a speck in his eye.

Draw a star in this box when you've read Matthew 7:3-5; Luke 6:41, 42.

Don't Judge

In Matthew 7:1, 2 and Luke 6:37, Jesus said not to judge. That means we shouldn't condemn people like a judge in a courtroom might do. Jesus said, "Don't judge, and you won't be judged. Don't condemn, and you won't be condemned. Forgive, and you'll be forgiven." One reason why we can't judge other people very well is that we don't know what's going on. It's hard to see to the heart of the matter. In I Samuel 16:7, God told Samuel that man looks on the outward appearance, but the Lord looks at the heart.

We Can't Judge Because It's Hard to See the Heart

Let's imagine that this kid is "judging" the situations. How do you think she sees each situation? What do you think is going on? *Find the hidden heart on each person this kid is judging. When you're done, look at the bottom of page 111 to see what the real circumstances were.*

1. Find the heart of the pastor entering the liquor store.

2. Find the heart of the man hitting his son.

3. Find the heart of the girl sticking a doll in her purse at the store.

4. Find the hearts of the girls who look like they're gossiping.

The Real Circumstances

1. The pastor's car broke down near the liquor store and he went in to call his wife.
2. The man was helping his son practice a scene from the school play.
3. The girl brought her own doll to the store to see what size clothes to buy for it.
4. The girls were talking about how happy the other girl would be when she found out about the surprise party they were planning for her.

Draw a star in this box when you've read Matthew 7:1, 2; Luke 6:37.

Make a Pointing Finger Mobile

When you point a finger at someone else, what do you have pointing back at you? Three fingers! When we criticize other people, we are sometimes more guilty than they are. Next time you start thinking about what's wrong with someone else, stop and see what you need to work on instead.

Make a pointing finger mobile to remind you that three fingers are pointing at you when you point at someone else.

What You Need

- poster board scraps
- markers
- scissors
- glue
- leftover sewing decorations (sequins, gold cord, etc.)
- paper hole punch
- twine or ribbon
- two coat hangers
- grown-up help

What You Do

1. *With a marker, trace your hand five times on pieces of poster board. Cut out the handprints, and draw details like fingernails on the hands. If you'd like, glue on the sewing decorations for jewelry.*

2. *Punch a hole at the bottom of the thumb of each handprint.*

3. *Make the handprints look like they are pointing by bending the middle finger, ring finger, and little finger where the knuckles would be.*

4. *Bend two coat hangers into the shape that's shown in the illustration.*

5. *Tie the handprints so they dangle from the four corners and middle of the mobile.*

6. *Hang the mobile by tying a thread from the hook at the top of the mobile.*

The Two Men at the Temple

In Luke 18:9-14, Jesus told a story about two men. One was a proud religious leader (called a "Pharisee"); the other was a humble man who knew he was a sinner. As you read this story, think about this: Are you more like the proud, religious leader or the humble man? *To read the story, change each letter to the letter that follows it in the alphabet. Change the letter Z to A.*

Idrtr rzhc svn ldm vdms sn sgd sdlokd sn opzx. Nmf vzr z Ogzqhrdd; sgd

nsgdq z szw bnkkdbsnq. Sgd Ogzqhrdd rsnnc zmc oqzxdc zants ghlrdke.

Gd rzhc, "Fnc, H sgzmj Xnt sgzs H zl mns khjd nsgdqr—bgdzsdqr zmc

duhkcndqr—nq dudm khjd sghr szw bnkkdbsnq. H cn fnnc sghmfr khjd

ezrshmf zmc fhuhmf z sdmsg ne dudqxsghmf H nvm sn sgd bgtqbg."

Sgd szw bnkkdbsnq vzr snn zrgzldc ne ghr rhmr sn khes ghr dxdr sn Fnc.

Gd ghs ghr bgdrs zmc rzhc, "Fnc, okdzrd enqfhud ld dudm sgntfg H cnm's

cdrdqud hs. H'l z rhmmdq."

Idrtr rzhc sgd szw bnkkdbsnq vzr enqfhudm ats sgd Ogzqhrdd vzrm's.

Zmxnmd vgn oteer ghlrdke to vhsg oqhcd vhkk ad gtlakdc zmc gd vgn

gtlakdr ghlrdke vhkk ad khesdc to sn khud vhsg Fnc.

☐ *Draw a star in this box when you've read Luke 18:9-14.*

Blessed Are the Peacemakers

In Matthew 5:9, Jesus said that peacemakers are blessed because they will be called the children of God. What does it mean to be a peacemaker? A peacemaker is someone who helps others get along. A peacemaker doesn't look for trouble or pick fights. A peacemaker settles arguments fairly and forgives others. Are you a peacemaker? *Unscramble these words to discover more traits of a peacemaker. Circle the ones that describe you.*

1. SOED ONT GHIFT
2. HEPLS OTHRES EGT LOAGN
3. SPERECTS HTORES
4. HOSWS VOLE
5. SERAC OHW THOERS EELF
6. SKAEPS NIKDYL
7. TASYS LACM

Stay as "Cool as a Cucumber"

Have you ever heard the expression "cool as a cucumber"? It means that a person doesn't let his or her temper get hot. When you feel yourself getting angry, try to calm down first. Take a deep breath and when you breathe out, ask God to help you be a peacemaker and stay as cool as a cucumber.

Make a Cool Cucumber Man to Eat

What You Need
• cucumber • carrot • potato peeler • raisins • pimento slice or small slice of cheese

What You Do

1. Using a potato peeler, peel the cucumber and a carrot. Then cut holes in the cucumber for eyes, arms, and legs. Also cut a notch in the cucumber for a mouth

2. Cut the carrot into four sticks. Poke the carrot sticks into the arm and leg holes. Press raisins into the eyeholes. Push a pimento slice or a small piece of sliced cheese into the mouth slit.

Draw a star in this box when you've read Matthew 5:9.

Be a Peacemaker for Your Country

A person who is a peacemaker tries to understand people and their situations. A peacemaker accepts others even if they are different. One way to be a peacemaker with people of other countries is to become a pen pal.

For free information about becoming a pen pal, you can write to the Student Letter Exchange at the address on the envelope below. Be sure to include your name, age, whether you're a boy or a girl, and a self-addressed, stamped envelope.

Student Letter Exchange
215 5th Avenue, S.E.
Waseca, MN 56093

Watch Your Words

Jesus said that on the Judgment Day, we will have to explain every careless word we have said. He doesn't want us to be angry with people or call them names. If we really love Jesus and follow Him, we will love other people. What we say <u>about</u> them and <u>to</u> them shows whether we actually love them.

Make Sweet Words to Eat

Have you ever heard someone say that you may have to "eat your words"? It means that you might have to "swallow" things you've said for one reason or another. If your words are sweet, however, you won't mind eating them.

First, unscramble the letters to discover some good advice. Then follow the recipe to make these letters out of dough. Eat your words and share them with others.

PEKE OURY RDOWS EWSTE

Letter Dough Recipe

What You Need

- 1/2 cup softened margarine
- 1/2 cup peanut butter
- 1/2 cup granulated sugar
- 1/2 cup brown sugar
- 1/2 teaspoon vanilla
- 1 1/4 cups all-purpose sifted flour

What You Do

1. *Mix the ingredients together in a bowl to make a dough. Shape the dough into letters.*
2. *Spell out the good advice and then eat your words, sharing the letters with other people.*

Draw a star in this box when you've read Matthew 5:21, 22; 12:36, 37.

Give and Lend

People are much more important than things. When you love people, you care more about them than your belongings. Jesus said we should give to people who ask and not say no to people who want to borrow things. Jesus also said not to ask for things back. When you give, it will be given back to you like a measuring cup that is pressed down, shaken together to make room for more, and running over.

Help Hoarding Horace Give

Horace has much more than he needs. Whenever you see an extra of anything in his room, circle it. Can you find ten extra objects for Horace to give away?

Do you have things you can give away? *Sort through your things to find items you don't need. Ask your parents if you can give these items to others who might like to have them.*

☐ *Draw a star in this box when you've read Matthew 5:40-42; and Luke 6:27-38.*

Go the Extra Mile

In Matthew 5:41, Jesus said that if someone makes you go a mile, you should go two. In other words, do more for that person than he or she asked.

Here's a practical way you can belong to the "extra mile club." *Every time one of your parents gives you a chore, do it right away and do a little more than they asked. Each time you do something they tell you to do, color in a square. If you "go the extra mile," color in another square. How many days will it take you to reach the extra mile club?*

Draw a star in this box when you've read Matthew 5:41.

Marriage

Jesus wants you to love everyone, especially the person you marry. When a man and woman marry, God joins them together and they become one. It's not God's plan for people who marry to split up.

Even though you're young, and marriage seems far away, now is a good time to decide that when you grow up and if you get married, you'll always work at loving the person you married.

Make a Colored Rice Picture

One wedding custom is to throw rice at the bride and groom as they leave the church after their wedding. *Glue colored rice onto this heart to decorate it.*

What You Need
- one cup Minute Rice
- four paper cups
- water
- food coloring
- glue
- paper towels

What You Do

1. Pour 1/4 cup of rice into each cup. Add only enough water to dampen the rice. Stir.
2. Stir in two drops of food coloring into each cup.
3. Drain off any extra water. Dry the rice on paper towels.
4. Glue the rice to the heart.

☐ *Draw a star in this box when you've read Matthew 5:31, 32; 19:3-9 and Mark 10:2-12.*

Just for Fun—Pretend You're Married

It's fun to imagine what you'll be like when you grow up. Here is a chance to play using some fun props. As you play, think about how you might solve problems that come up in real families.

Make a Bride's Hair and Veil

What You Need

- medium-size paper bag
- sheer curtain or piece of netting
- scissors
- stapler and staples

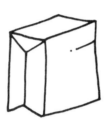

What You Do

1. *Cut a medium-size paper bag as shown in this illustration.*
2. *Use one blade of a pair of scissors to curl the hair.*
3. *Staple a piece of a sheer curtain or a piece of netting to the paper bag wig.*

Make Flowers for the Bride's Bouquet and the Groom's Boutonniere

What You Need

- facial tissue
- scissors
- wire or thread

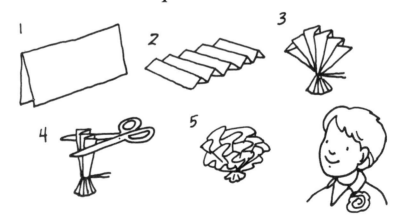

What You Do

1. *Fold a facial tissue in half the long way. Make 1/2-inch pleats. Cut off the folded edge.*
2. *Tie the center with wire or thread. Carefully pull apart the tissues.*

Make a Paper Beard

What You Need

- paper bag
- scissors
- string

What You Do

1. *Cut a paper bag into a beard as shown in the illustration. Cut the slits to look like hair.*
2. *Curl the "hair" using one blade of the scissors.*
3. *Poke a hole on each side of the beard. Tie a string through each hole. Put the beard over your mouth, and use the strings to tie it around your head.*

Make Poster Board People Puppets

What You Need

- poster boards
- pencil and markers
- scissors

What You Do

1. *Draw a circle slightly bigger than your face. Cut it out.*
2. *Draw clothes on the poster boards. If you want to, decorate them with colored paper or fabric scraps and sewing decorations.*
3. *Poke your head through the hole and pretend you're grown up.*

Here are some other suggestions for things to use as you pretend (ask permission first): curlers, old colored stockings, adult shoes, adult clothes, sunglasses, and a car made from a big box with a steering wheel and tires made of paper plates taped to the box.

Jesus Gives You a New Heart

Have you asked Jesus to be your Savior and Lord? Do you know what that means? When you ask Jesus to be your Savior, you are trusting Him to save you from punishment you deserve after you die for the wrong things you've done. You are saying you believe He already took the punishment for you. When you ask Jesus to be your Lord, you're asking Him to lead you and you're promising to try to follow Him. If you haven't asked Jesus to be your Savior and Lord yet, please do it right now.

In Ezekiel 36:26 the Lord promised, "I will remove from you your heart of stone and give you a heart of flesh." A stony heart is cold and unfeeling. It's hard to love with that kind of heart. When you trust Jesus as your Savior and follow Him as your Lord, He gives you a heart filled with love for others.

Make New Heart "Stained-Glass" Cookies

What You Need

- chilled sugar cookie dough (store-bought or homemade)
- red, clear, hard candies or lollipops
- plastic bag
- hammer
- aluminum foil
- cookie sheet
- grown-up help

What You Do

1. *Preheat oven according to the directions for the cookie dough.*
2. *Line cookie sheet with foil.*
3. *Put candies in a plastic bag. Tap them with the hammer gently until they are in small pieces (but not complete crushed into powder). Set aside.*
4. *Roll cookie dough into long ropes as thin as you can get them (about 1/4" thick). Shape the ropes into hearts on the cookie sheets. Be sure the pieces connect well.*
5. *Sprinkle the pieces of candy into the centers of the hearts.*
6. *Bake until the cookies brown slightly and the candies melt. Be careful not to overcook.*
7. *Remove the pan from the oven. When the cookies are cool, carefully pull the foil off the back of each. As you eat the cookies, thank Jesus for changing your heart.*

Draw a star in this box when you've read Ezekiel 36:26.

Give Your Heart

Here are some fun ways to show your love for others. Put your heart into making these projects for other people.

Heart Art to Decorate a Kind Note

What You Need

- red stamp pad or plate with red paint
- white construction paper for the note card

Fingerprint Hearts

What You Do

Press your index finger on a red stamp pad or a plate with red paint. Then slant your finger as you press it onto paper to make hearts. Write notes to friends, parents, and teachers, letting them know how much you appreciate them.

Potpourri Heart

What You Need

- clean Styrofoam meat tray
- potpourri
- paper clip
- duct tape
- white construction paper for the note card

What You Do

1. *Cut a heart shape from a clean Styrofoam meat tray. Spread glue on it, and sprinkle it with potpourri.*
2. *Use duct tape to attach a paper clip to the back for hanging the tray. Make a small loop of duct tape to attach the heart to a card. When you give the card to someone you love, mention that the heart can be pulled off and hung on the wall.*

Give Your Heart

Gelatin Hearts

What You Need

- two 3-oz. packages of strawberry or cherry gelatin
- one cup boiling water
- 9-inch square baking dish
- heart-shaped cookie cutter
- spatula

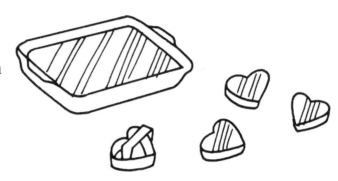

What You Do

1. Mix two 3-oz. packages of strawberry or cherry gelatin with one cup of boiling water. Stir until dissolved and pour into a square 9-inch baking dish.
2. When the gelatin is firm, cut out heart shapes with the cookie cutter. Remove the hearts from the dish with the spatula.

A "Heart-y" Meal

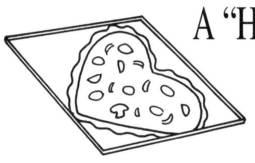

Offer to help your mom make a meal. See if you can find ways to add hearts to whatever she is fixing. You could cut cheese chunks or carrot slices into hearts for a salad. You could cut strawberry or banana slices into hearts. You could shape a pizza or meat loaf into a heart. Be creative.

Painted Cupcakes

Simply dip a clean watercolor brush into one or two drops of food coloring and paint hearts on frosted cupcakes. Give the cupcakes to people you love.

I Did It!

COMPLETED	DATE	COMPLETED	DATE
☐ A New Commandment	_____	☐ Make Up Quickly	_____
☐ Make a Tin Punch Pie Plate	_____	☐ Love Everyone . . .	_____
☐ The Golden Rule	_____	☐ The Good News	_____
☐ Practice the Golden Rule	_____	☐ Jesus Ate with Sinners	_____
☐ The Good Samaritan	_____	☐ The Speck and the Plank	_____
☐ Tell the Good Samaritan Story with Puppets	_____	☐ Don't Judge	_____
☐ Love Your Neighbor as Yourself	_____	☐ Make a Pointing Finger Mobile	_____
☐ Include Others	_____	☐ The Two Men at the Temple	_____
☐ The Least of These	_____	☐ Blessed Are the Peacemakers	_____
☐ Help Others and Help Jesus	_____	☐ Watch Your Words	_____
☐ Jesus Washed His Disciples' Feet	_____	☐ Give and Lend	_____
☐ Jump at the Chance to Serve God	_____	☐ Go the Extra Mile	_____
☐ The Forgiven Servant Who Didn't Forgive	_____	☐ Just for Fun, Pretend You're Married	_____
☐ Erase Unforgiveness from Your Heart	_____	☐ Jesus Gives You a New Heart	_____
☐ Unlimited Forgiveness	_____	☐ Give Your Heart	_____

Answers

Page 7 **Page 8**

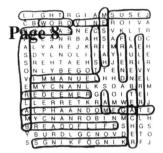

1. Savior; 2. Messiah; 3. Bread of Life; 4. Friend;
5. God; 6. Lord; 7. Lamb of God; 8. King of Kings;
9. Word; 10. Redeemer

Page 10 1. People want to know God and be sure they will get to live with Him forever. When they put their trust in Jesus, He satisfies that hunger like the manna satisfied the hunger of the Israelites.

2. The Israelites would have died if God had not sent manna. We would all die for eternity if God had not sent Jesus.

3. The Israelites had to collect their manna every day. We need to pray every day and keep trusting in Jesus.

Page 12 1. service; 2. lamps; 3. wedding; 4. knocks; 5. door; 6. servants; 7. watching; 8. table; 9. good; 10. master

Page 14 The kingdom of heaven is like (ten) young women who took their lamps and went to meet the bridegroom. Five of them were (wise) and five were foolish. The foolish ones brought lamps without extra (oil), but the wise brought oil with their lamps. They all fell (asleep) waiting for the bridegroom. At midnight someone yelled, "The bridegroom is coming. (Go) out to meet him." All the (young) women got up and cut the wicks on their lamps. The foolish ones asked the wise ones for some (oil), but the wise women couldn't give them any because there would not be enough (for) everyone. The foolish young women left to buy some (oil). While they were gone, the bridegroom (came). The ones who were ready went inside for the wedding, and the (door) was shut behind them. When the foolish young women returned, (the) bridegroom didn't let them inside. He said, "I don't know you." Jesus said for us to watch because we don't know the (day) or hour when He'll come.

Page 17 Beginning with top left picture: 1. James; 2. John; 3. Thomas; 4. Matthew; 5. Paul; 6. Elijah; 7. Jonah; 8. Daniel; 9. John; 10. Peter; 11. Jesus; 12. Noah; 13. Joseph; 14. Moses; 15. David

Page 18 1. Jesus said, "I have called you friends."

2. If you feel too guilty to pray, remember: Jesus was a friend of sinners.

3. Jesus showed how greatly He loves you, His friend, when He gave His life for you.

4. You are never alone because Jesus said, "I am with you always."

Answers

Page 19   No man comes to the Father except through me.

Page 20   "Trusting Jesus as my way to heaven will save me." should be taped on the door.

Page 21   1. The gift of God; 2. He loved the world; 3. Eternal life; 4. Too wonderful for words

Page 22   Hidden name: I AM; 1. - 1; 2. - =

Page 23   God with us

Page 24   1. Joshua; 2. Angel; 3. Salvation; 4. Paul; 5. Saved

Pages 26-27   1. A; 2. C; 3. F; 4. I; 5. H; 6. J; 7. D; 8. B; 9. 3; 10. G; 11. K

Page 31

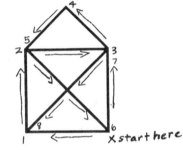

Page 33   Anointed One; 1. Bethlehem; 2. Donkey; 3. Cross; 4. Robbers; 5. Vinegar; 6. Dead

Page 34   1. Forgave his sins; 2. Lazarus, The son of a widow, The daughter of Jairus;
3. Bartimaeus; 4. Fever; 5. Thank Him

Page 36   I will live again after my body dies because of Jesus.

Page 37

Page 41   1. day; 2. up; 3. sun; 4. white; 5. Old; 6. appeared; 7. death;
8. good; 9. here; 10. he; 11. bright; 12. on; 13. up

Page 42   I am the vine; you are the branches. If a man remains in me and I in him, he will bear much fruit; apart from me you can do nothing. My followers produce a lot of fruit. This gives glory to my Father.

Page 44   1. False
2. True
3. True
4. False

Answers

Page 49 Believe in Jesus
He who stands firm to the end will be saved.

Page 54 Enter through the narrow gate. For wide is the gate and broad is the road that leads to destruction, and many enter through it. But small is the gate and narrow the road that leads to life, and only a few find it.

Page 55 Jesus didn't come to patch up or add to the old ways (the law). He came to bring a new way (grace).

Page 58 Bad News: None of us deserve to live with God because we have all sinned.
Good News: If we have faith in Jesus, our sins are forgiven and we will live with God.

Page 61 God's grace is more than anyone deserves, and He gives it the same to all who enter His kingdom.

Page 62 Brighten the world around you by letting people see Jesus in you.

Page 63 1. Give a big smile; 2. Tell about Jesus; 3. Offer to help people; 4. Forgive others

Page 65

Page 66

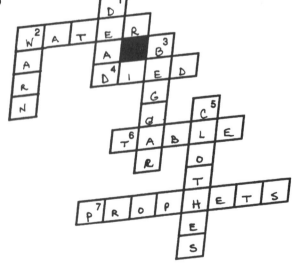

Answers

Page 68 I will serve God with my money.

Page 69 You cannot serve both God and money.

Page 70 Your heart will be where your treasure is.

Page 71 1. Some feel they do not need God. 2. Some think they are better than other people. 3. Some will not share with others. 4. Some do not let God use their money how He wants.

Page 72 Camels: You obey picky little laws but disobey God in big ways.
Dishes: To be truly good, people must have their hearts changed by Jesus.
Bones: They did not believe in Jesus.

Page 73 Anything you hide will be shown later. What you say in the dark will be heard in the daylight. What you whisper in your room will be yelled from the roof.

Page 74

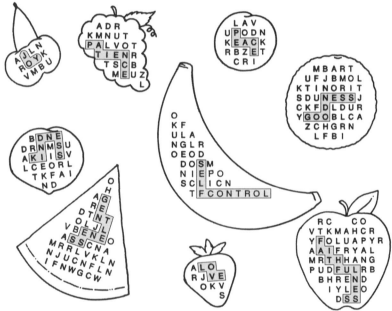

Page 75 1-A; 2-C; 3-D; 4-B

Page 76 If a blind man leads a blind man, both will fall into a pit.

Page 77 Bear - yes; Hen - yes; Elephant - no; Goat - yes; Kangaroo - no; Lion - yes

Page 78 Do not be too busy to learn from the Lord.

Page 81 What do I need to get rid of to keep from sinning?

Page 82 14 marshmallows; 25 toothpicks

Page 83 Decide to serve Jesus and then don't slow down or stop. Don't ever think about going back to the life you had before you asked Jesus to be your Lord.

Page 84 1. People; 2. God's

Answers

Page 98 The Son of God will sit on a throne and say to some of the people, "Come, you who are blessed by My Father, inherit a kingdom that was prepared for you when the world was created. I was hungry and you gave Me something to eat. I was thirsty and you gave Me something to drink. I was a stranger and you invited Me in. I was naked and you clothed Me. I was sick and you looked after Me. I was in prison and you came to Me."

Then those who are righteous will say, "When did we do those things for You?" The King will answer, "When you did it for the least of My brothers, you did it for Me."

Jesus said the others will be punished for not helping Him when He was in need. They'll say, "When did we see You in need and we didn't help You?" He'll say, "When you didn't help the least of My brothers, you didn't help Me." Jesus said those who didn't help Him will go to everlasting punishment, but those who were righteous will go to live with God forever.

Page 102 God has forgiven us.

Page 104

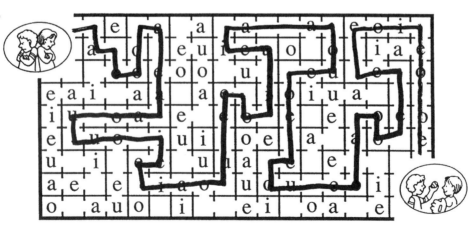

1. Pray for God to take away your unforgiveness.
2. Think about why the person did what she did.
3. Talk about the problem when you're both calm.
4. Try to love the person like God does.

Answers

Page 110 1. Heart is on his shoe
2. Heart is in his hair
3. Heart is on her left-hand sleeve
4. Heart is on button of the girl on the right-hand side

Page 113 Jesus said two men went to the temple to pray. One was a Pharisee; the other a tax collector. The Pharisee stood and prayed about himself. He said, "God, I thank You that I am not like other men–cheaters and evildoers–or even like this tax collector. I do good things like fasting and giving a tenth of everything I own to the church."

The tax collector was too ashamed of his sins to lift his eyes to God. He hit his chest and said, "God, please forgive me even though I don't deserve it. I'm a sinner."

Jesus said the tax collector was forgiven but the Pharisee wasn't. Anyone who puffs himself up with pride will be humbled and he who humbles himself will be lifted up to God.

Page 114 1. Does not fight
2. Helps others get along
3. Respects others
4. Shows love
5. Cares how others feel
6. Speaks kindly
7. Stays calm

Page 116 keep your words sweet

Page 117 teddy bear, frog, piggy bank, tennis racket, jacket, hat, fishing pole, ball, water gun, baseball bat

Index

VOLUMES

Volume 1
Jesus' Early Years

Jesus Is Born

Jesus Grows Up

Jesus Prepares to Serve

Volume 2
Jesus' Ministry

Jesus Works Miracles

Jesus Heals

Jesus Teaches Me
to Pray

Volume 3
Following Jesus

Names of Jesus

Following Jesus

Learning to Love
Like Jesus

Volume 4
The Love of Jesus

Jesus Shows God's Love

Jesus' Last Week

Jesus Is Alive!

BIBLE STORY	LIFE AND LESSONS	BIBLE STORY	LIFE AND LESSONS
Healing of:		Jesus Is:	
10 Lepers	Vol. 2	the Light	Vol. 3
Blind Man	Vol. 3	the Redeemer	Vol. 3
Deaf and Mute Man	Vol. 3	the Resurrection and Life	Vol. 3
A Leper	Vol. 2	the Savior	Vol. 3
A Man's Hand	Vol. 2	the Son of God	Vol. 3
Blind Bartimaeus	Vol. 2	the Truth	Vol. 3
Centurion's Servant	Vol. 2	the Vine	Vol. 3
Epileptic Boy	Vol. 2	the Way	Vols. 3, 4
Malchus's Ear	Vol. 2	the Word	Vol. 3
Man Born Blind	Vol. 3	Jesus Loves Children	Vol. 4
Man with Dropsy	Vol. 2	Jesus Obeys Parents	Vol. 1
Official's Son	Vol. 2	Jesus Prayed	Vol. 2
Peter's Mother-in-Law	Vol. 2	Jesus Shows Compassion	Vol. 4
Paralytic	Vol. 2	Jesus Washes Disciples' Feet	Vols. 3, 4
Woman's Back	Vol. 2	Jesus' Family	Vol. 1
Woman Who Touched Hem	Vol. 2	Jesus' Genealogy	Vol. 1
Heaven	Vol. 4	Jesus' Trial Before Caiaphas	Vol. 4
How Much God Loves Us	Vol. 4	Jesus' Trial Before Pilate	Vol. 4
Humble Prayer	Vol. 2	John the Baptist	Vol. 1
I		Joseph's Dream	Vol. 1
I Am with You Always	Vol. 4	Judas Betrays Jesus	Vols. 1, 4
I Live/You Will Live	Vol. 4	Judge Not	Vol. 3
Include Others	Vol. 3	**K**	
J		Known by Fruits	Vol. 3
Jesus Clears the Temple	Vol. 4	**L**	
Jesus Died for Me	Vol. 4	Last Supper	Vol. 4
Jesus Eats with Sinners	Vol. 4	Lay Down Life for Friends	Vols. 3, 4
Jesus Has Overcome the World	Vol. 4	Lazarus and the Rich Man	Vol. 3
Jesus Is:		Life in New Testament Times	Vol. 1
'I AM'	Vol. 3	Light on a Hill	Vol. 3
Arrested	Vol. 4	Like Days of Noah	Vol. 4
Born	Vol. 1	Like Jonah's Three Days in Fish	Vol. 4
Buried	Vol. 4	Lord's Prayer	Vol. 2
Christ	Vols. 1, 3	Love Each Other	Vol. 4
Crucified and Dies	Vol. 4	Love Jesus Most	Vol. 4
God	Vol. 3	Love Me/Obey Me	Vol. 4
Immanuel	Vol. 3	Love One Another	Vol. 3
Tempted	Vol. 1	Loving Enemies	Vols. 2, 3
the Bread of Life	Vol. 3	**M**	
the Bridegroom	Vol. 3	Make Up Quickly	Vol. 3
the Chief Cornerstone	Vol. 3	Maps of New Testament Times	Vols. 1, 2
the Gate	Vol. 3	Mary and Martha	Vol. 3
the Gift of God	Vol. 3	Mary Anoints Jesus with Perfume	Vol. 4
the Good Shepherd	Vol. 3	Mary Visits Elizabeth	Vol. 1
the Lamb of God	Vol. 3		

N		S	
Name the Baby Jesus	Vol. 3	Salt of the Earth	Vol. 3
Narrow Road	Vol. 3	Second Coming	Vol. 4
New Commandment: Love	Vol. 3	Seek Kingdom First	Vol. 2
Nicodemus	Vol. 3	Seventy Times Seven	Vol. 3
Not Left As Orphans	Vol. 4	Sheep Know His Voice	Vol. 2
O		Shepherd Knows Sheep	Vol. 4
Old and New Cloth	Vol. 3	Speck and the Plank	Vol. 3
Oxen in a Pit	Vol. 2	Spiritual Harvest	Vol. 3
P		T	
Parable of:		Take Up Your Cross	Vol. 4
the Friend at Midnight	Vol. 2	Thief in the Night	Vol. 4
the Good Samaritan	Vol. 3	Thomas Sees Resurrected Jesus	Vol. 4
the Lost Coin	Vol. 4	Transfiguration	Vol. 1
the Lost Sheep	Vol. 4	Treasure in Heaven	Vol. 3
the Overpaid Workers	Vol. 3	Triumphal Entry	Vol. 4
the Persistent Widow	Vol. 2	True Members of Jesus' Family	Vol. 1
the Prodigal Son	Vols. 2, 3	Truth Makes You Free	Vol. 3
the Sheep and Goats	Vols. 3, 4	Twelve Disciples	Vol. 1
Sower and Seeds	Vols. 3, 4	Two Agree in Prayer	Vol. 2
the Ten Young Women	Vol. 3	U	
the Unforgiving Servant	Vol. 3	Under His Wing	Vol. 4
Wedding Feast	Vol. 3	V	
Weeds	Vol. 4	Vine and Branches	Vol. 3
Wise and Foolish Builders	Vol. 3	W	
Mustard Seed and Leaven	Vols. 3, 4	Walking on Water	Vol. 2
Treasure, Pearl, Fishnet	Vols. 3, 4	Water to Wine	Vol. 2
Passover	Vols. 1, 3, 4	What Makes a Person Unclean	Vol. 3
Peter's Denial	Vols. 1, 4	Widow's Mites	Vol. 3
Pharisee and Tax Collector at Temple	Vol. 3	Wine and Wineskins	Vol. 3
Pharisees' Hypocrisy	Vol. 3	Wise Men Visit Jesus	Vol. 1
Pray Always	Vol. 2	Withered Fig Tree	Vol. 2
Prepare a Place for You	Vol. 4	Wolves in Sheep's Clothing	Vol. 3
Promise of Holy Spirit	Vol. 4	Woman at the Well	Vol. 3
R		Woman Caught Sinning	Vol. 3
Raising of Jairus's Daughter	Vol. 2	Worth More than Sparrows	Vol. 4
Raising of Lazarus	Vol. 2	Y	
Raising of Widow's Son	Vol. 2	Yoke Easy, Burden Light	Vol. 2
Rich Toward God	Vol. 3	Z	
Rich Young Ruler	Vol. 3	Zacchaeus	Vol. 4
Road to Emmaus	Vol. 4		